The Viking's Guide
To Pillaging the Real World

The Journey of Mad Hadley

A QUICK NOTE FROM THE AUTHOR

I've had the good fortune to associate with an extraordinary cast of characters including CEOs, pilots, firefighters, doctors, attorneys, tradesmen, businessmen and businesswomen, farmers, ranchers, miners, writers, teachers, law enforcement officers, and military personnel of the highest caliber. In their own right they are all highly successful and respected people—and many of them are considered the best in their chosen field. They are simply people who have found their own path and travelled it well, and that's what this book is about.

As for me, I've had a good run in some very competitive and challenging professions. I've been a U.S. Forest Service Smokejumper, a firefighter in a major metropolitan department, and a pilot at a major airline. Somehow, I always found a way to buck the odds and make the grade—regardless of an apparent lack of talent and ability.

That being said, I do possess one very natural gift: I am an exceptional observer. I have the quiet habit of paying attention to everyone and everything, and that habit ultimately created this book. Great victories, crushing defeats, and lessons learned from exceptional people have all given rise to Mad Hadley, Feral Dave, Olga the She-Bear, and their Norse associates.

The Viking's Guide to Pillaging the Real World - The Journey of Mad Hadley is a story about how people succeed, fail, and define themselves in a very competitive and challenging world. It's about pursuing *your* life and *your* career, and how to find what *you* really value along the way. I hope you enjoy it, and most of all, I hope you find something in this Viking adventure that speaks to you.

This book is dedicated to the real world.

You've been a strict coach and a patient teacher,
and for that I am eternally grateful.

CONTENTS

PART III

WELCOME TO THE VIKING WORLD

THIS IS A story borne of extraordinary victories and grizzly defeats on the arduous and unpredictable battlefields of the real world. It is for those who want to walk their own path with the cunning and tenacity of an ancient Viking warrior, and for those who are not afraid of bearing down and doing what it really takes to find the top of their own mountain.

Whatever profession you choose, whether it requires a white collar, a blue collar, or a Viking helmet, the challenges are all of a surprisingly similar nature. Your path will undoubtedly be twisting, turning, and often rocky, and as your journey unfolds you will be confronted with ideas and beliefs both good and bad.

In order to successfully find your way, you will need to know which rules to follow and which rules to break. In this Norse odyssey we will trek through the dark forests of truth and fiction, wade the mire of ambiguity, and ultimately discover the ideas, beliefs, and rules that lead to genuine success. It's about discovering what is truly valuable, embracing challenge, and doing what is really right for you. Welcome to the Viking world.

PART I

BATTERED, BLOODY, AND DIRTY

THE NORDIC SUN is sinking into the deep blue sea as the weathered raiding ship slips through the mouth of the icy mountain fjord that is home. The brawny vessel is near the end of a punishing yet rewarding journey, and its heaving deck bears a battle-worn crew that possesses a gallant and excited energy. Proudly standing at the helm is a familiar face in these waters: Mad Hadley the Viking. He and his crew are returning from a grueling expedition in a faraway land, and they are feeling the deep satisfaction and pride of being battered, bloody, and dirty.

Some have black eyes, and some are missing a few teeth, but after just a few more miles the bruised but exuberant band of warriors will moor their treasure-laden boat at the village docks. Their Viking friends and families will greet them, and there will be a great feast that will carry into the wee hours of the Norse night. In the morning, they will count the gold, silver, and jewels in their cargo hold.

Along with their vast haul of precious metals and expensive baubles, the intrepid warriors have also returned with another precious commodity: the skills and experience that are borne only from great challenges. While it is true that all Vikings need financial resources to buy new ships, swords, and shields, it's their newly acquired abilities and knowledge that hold the greatest value because each of them will now be better equipped to handle the future challenges of Viking life.

However, there was a Viking named Frank who didn't care much for skills, challenges, or the future. He thought that raiding and pillaging were too much effort, and in general, hard work should be sidestepped at all costs. The sluggish Norseman thought it would be easiest to hang out on the beach and collect a few coins for unloading treasure from returning raiding ships, and even in performing this simple task he expended as little effort as possible. Frank avoided demanding jobs to live easy and carefree, but ironically his life was a continual struggle of sporadic employment and shaky finances, and sadly, his horns began to droop over time.

Unfortunately, there was an even bigger problem than Frank's droopy horns. He never gained the skills needed to handle the tough times, and in the Viking world the next trial was usually lurking just around the corner. One day a savage horde came thundering down the road to raid the village, and Frank, being unskilled and defenseless, was the first to get his head lopped off. He had no capabilities and no experience, and hence, no chance. The experienced Vikings who had challenged themselves in the past were able to defend themselves, and they all happily lived to fight another day.

For his entire life, Frank avoided challenges and took the easy way out. He thought he would live a long and happy life by avoiding the fray and dodging responsibility, but instead he endured a short and miserable existence. The pathetic Norseman never experienced the exuberance of a great Viking victory, and he never knew the satisfaction of rising to a challenge. On the other hand, Mad Hadley and his friends who survived the battle knew that facing challenges head on and getting battered, bloody, and dirty was the only way to survive and thrive in a tough Viking world.

THE PURE MAGIC OF INITIATIVE

IF CHALLENGE HAD a best Viking buddy, it would be the pure magic known as initiative. In other words, sometimes things simply needed to be done, and each Viking needed to do these things on their own. Initiative was everything in the Viking world and without it nothing would have ever been accomplished, but it was initiative that repeatedly escaped the attention of a Viking named Morty.

Morty usually did an adequate job and was able to keep his head during the big battle in the village, but, for some reason, he never got promoted up the Viking ladder like he wanted. He silently fumed about his lack of advancement, but he never realized the need to take the initiative to do things on his own. Sure, he performed necessary duties like sharpening his sword and slaying the occasional warrior from a distant village, but he always had to be directed to do other things that obviously needed to be done. Viking tools like battle axes with broken handles often needed fixing, but Morty would not fix anything until he was told to do so, and even then he was usually resentful about doing anything that went above and beyond.

The oblivious Morty also failed to take the initiative to learn new things and to grow to his fullest Viking potential, and this was a tragic waste since he lived in a world of infinite educational resources. The local Viking college offered a myriad of courses like Advanced Mayhem and Chaos Theory for Future Viking Leaders, but the lackadaisical Norseman never took the time to attend. He thought that swinging a sword was a good enough skill set, and it most certainly was for someone who just wanted to swing a sword as a career. Morty just didn't understand that he had to take the initiative to turn himself into a better Viking to get promoted.

Hadley, however, knew about initiative. He showed up early and stayed late when things needed to be done, and he also knew how to take care of things on his own. The enthusiastic Viking started his working life as a barnacle scraper in the Viking shipyards and did his job to the utmost of his ability, and he also cleaned the scraping equipment every week even though nobody told him to do so. The energetic warrior also took the initiative to fix broken battle axe handles and to wash the blood off of the decks of returning raiding ships, and he always did so without complaint. Of course, Hadley never overstepped his bounds by delving into things above his pay grade, but he always took the initiative to do what obviously needed to be done.

Being a highly motivated Viking, Hadley also exercised initiative in educating himself. Upon becoming a newly minted raider, he learned all he could about the seas he would sail and the villages he would pillage. He often devoted nights and weekends to some course of self-improvement, and Hadley could always be found with his nose in a book that would help him to become an official fearsome Viking warrior. He attained a high degree of competence and knowledge, and the determined Hadley knew that he had to earn these skills and abilities on his own.

Mad Hadley eventually grew to be a great warrior as well as a leader. He exercised initiative time and again by taking care of the little things, and he made sure to take the initiative to become a better Viking as well. He gained respect and credibility, and in time he was made a Viking captain and given his own ship—all because of the pure magic of initiative.

EXCELLENCE IS VICTORY, MEDIOCRITY IS DEFEAT

OTHER THAN TAKING initiative to get things done, Hadley also got things done with excellence. If he was scraping barnacles, then he was scraping them as thoroughly and efficiently as possible. When he became a Viking warrior he did everything with focus and purpose, and as a captain all of his raids were carried out with precise effect. Each and every job, big and small, was done with excellence, and that would lead to victory time and again. On the other hand, there were also those that strove only for mediocrity, and they would taste the bitterness of defeat just as often.

Opportunity often appeared out of the blue Norse sky, and one day in his early Viking career, it did so for Hadley. The very young and inexperienced warrior was suddenly presented with an opportunity to go on an important raid in a faraway land, and it was the type of raid that could make or break a new warrior. Fortunately, Mad Hadley was ready. While he remained modest because he had little real world experience, the young raider was still self-assured and bold because he had approached his training with the right attitude. Mad Hadley possessed a humble confidence that could only be wrought from an attitude of excellence, and that attitude would soon pay off.

After a few days of smooth sailing, the voyagers met stormy seas. As they pitched and crashed through the waves, Hadley

handled himself with skill and poise. Once they made landfall and the mayhem of battle began, it was the same. Hadley
acted with bravery and cunning and pillaged well, and in the
end, he returned home with a really big pile of loot. By the end
of the voyage, Mad Hadley had earned the respect of his fellow
Vikings, and he also began to build a reputation that would last
for the rest of his career.

There was another new warrior on the voyage named Vinny.
He was the charismatic half-brother of Morty and was liked by
everybody but trusted by no one. He had failed to earn trust
and respect because he was a mediocre warrior who talked
more than he acted. The unmotivated slacker was always chat-
tering about battle ax practice and sailing lessons, but he never
fully engaged in either of these. In fact, he rarely put more than a
mediocre effort into anything.

As often happens with such characters, Vinny was able to
feign competence just well enough to fool the Big Chiefs into
letting him go on the voyage. At first, he was able to pull his
weight and he was even liked well enough by the crew, but big
problems emerged when they hit stormy seas and Vinny's mediocre preparation began to show. He didn't handle the pressure
of the great ocean storms because his own attitude toward sailing lessons had been lax, and his poor performance in the storm
endangered the lives of his fellow Vikings. Worse yet, Vinny still
failed to learn the lesson that the sea was trying to teach him:
Mediocrity taught him to sail on smooth waters, but rising to
excellence was the only way to handle the storm.

Vinny's problems got even bigger on the first day of pillaging and mayhem. He was so unprepared for the chaos and inten-
sity of battle that he eventually hid behind a large boulder where
he cried and sucked his thumb until the battle was over. Of
course, this did not go unnoticed by the other Vikings who were
reluctant to allow him back on the ship because he had failed
the team in a monumental manner. Luckily for Vinny, there
were a few sympathetic warriors who didn't think he deserved

abandonment on enemy shores, but he was only allowed back on the ship to serve as the bathroom attendant for the entire journey home.

Like all successful Vikings, Mad Hadley strove for excellence in everything, and it paid off when the going got tough. He savored the sweetness of victory while Vinny floundered in incompetence, and in the end, they both proved the old Viking adage: excellence is victory, mediocrity is defeat.

ROW FOR ONE, ROW FOR ALL

HADLEY DID EVERYTHING with excellence, but there was something that drove him to it. Treasure, praise from the Big Chiefs, and even bragging rights were nice rewards, but they weren't always what drove him. While performing with excellence felt good, it still wasn't his sole motivation. There was something else…fear. Generally, Hadley was not fearful by nature, but he harbored a deep-seated fear of letting down the team, and that helped to drive the lion-hearted warrior to excellence. Deep down, Mad Hadley knew that he could not just row for one—he had to row for all.

Along with his inner angst about failing his teammates, Hadley also secretly dreaded something else: the Norse legend of the Colossal Rabid Sea Snake. The snake was reported to be a villainous beast that would smash ships with a flick of its tail and then swallow Vikings whole, but in reality, most considered the snake to be nothing more than a fanciful myth. Occasionally, life was breathed into the legend by Norsemen rescued from the sea who had allegedly experienced the wrath of the Colossal Rabid Sea Snake, although these reports were rare and unverified. In truth, most wrote them off to the vivid imaginations of Viking tabloid writers.

Mad Hadley kept his fear of the snake secret, but eventually his two fears would meet in a contest where only one could prevail. It was a clear Norse day as the young and inexperienced

Hadley ventured down the coast with a seasoned crew of steely-eyed warriors on a short and presumably easy Viking business trip. The wind had failed them and they couldn't run under the power of sail, so they were merrily rowing to their destination. The camaraderie, along with the warm sun and the tranquil sea, made it a great day to be a Viking. None of them would have traded it for anything in the world, but their peaceful, easy feelings were soon shattered as the blue sea was parted by a villainous serpentine head. The Colossal Rabid Sea Snake was real, and it was now rapidly bearing down on their small Viking craft.

Hadley's rowing partner was a capable Viking named Feral Dave. Dave was a tough and wily Viking who was also just learning the ropes of raiding and pillaging (R&P in the Viking world), and he was the first to see the frightful beast. As Dave sounded the alarm, a sense of impending doom coursed throughout the crew. But, after a brief moment of terror, they all realized there was only one way to survive this menace—as a team.

They dug their oars into the water knowing that they had to be in perfect sync with each other. One mistimed stroke would slow them all, and they knew that everyone had to give all they had. What they didn't know, but were about to realize through an epic display of teamwork, is that they all shared the same fear as Hadley: no one wanted to let the team down. Over the past several months, they had all prepared physically and mentally for this very moment without even knowing it.

Now here they were, rowing as a team because their lives depended on it. And row they did. With perfect synchronicity and the strength of angry bulls, they plowed through the salty sea toward a distant shore that was their only possible salvation. But to their dismay, the Sea Snake was gaining on them, and there was only one thing to do: become a greater team than anyone thought possible.

They stepped up the pace to a level few had ever experienced. Their arms burned with searing agony, and their backs felt like they were on fire, but now they were at least holding their own against the serpent. The crew was pushing themselves beyond the physical limits of mere mortal Vikings, and within the agony, they felt the beauty and power of real teamwork.

They were all verging on physical collapse as the nearly forsaken craft made landfall with a gigantic thump on a rocky beach. The Colossal Rabid Sea Snake was helpless on dry land, so it slithered back to the depths from which it came with nothing more than an evil glare at its missed dining opportunity. The crew reveled in its own survival, and Mad Hadley and Feral Dave learned that their willingness and ability to give everything for the team had earned the trust and respect of their Viking colleagues—something that was worth more than any pillaged treasure in the world. The Vikings lived to see another day because they were individuals who knew when to pull together as a team, and Mad Hadley and Feral Dave now knew full well the lesson of not just rowing for one, but rowing for all.

THE GOLDEN RULE OF REPUTATION

MAD HADLEY'S DRIVE for excellence was noticed by everyone in the Viking world. Sometimes it was mentioned to his boss, and sometimes it was discussed among his peers. Vikings talked about other Vikings, and they did so because their success in battle hinged upon knowing who was capable of smiting enemies and who would be found sucking their thumb behind a rock. The way in which Vikings were seen by their peers either opened doors to future opportunities or sank them into the sea of failure. This was the golden rule of reputation.

The evening before Hadley's first big battle, the would-be warrior stayed up late sharpening his battle ax and spreading a fresh layer of pine tar on the handle for a good solid Viking grip. He shined his shield and checked that his horns were solidly mounted and perfectly pointed. In fact, Hadley was so focused on being the best Viking raider he could possibly be that he wasn't aware that the other warriors—including the Big Chiefs—were taking notice of him. They noticed because they depended on him, and it was the Big Chiefs' job to know their men and everything about them. It did not go unnoticed that Hadley was an excellent pillager who was swift and brave on the battlefield, and his compatriots and leaders all witnessed acts of boldness and initiative time after time. Thus, Mad Hadley's reputation grew.

Morty never understood that people were always watching and always talking. He especially didn't understand that even though the Big Chiefs were always wrapped up in meetings and other things of great importance, they were still paying attention to their young Viking warriors. By knowing each warrior and their reputation, a Viking Big Chief could discern who would perform in battle, who would be a future leader, and who might someday stick a knife in their back. Regrettably, Morty continually failed to comprehend that reputation was the mysterious force that maneuvered his Viking career.

On the other hand, his half-brother Vinny did understand that people watched and talked, but he didn't understand that reputations are made of authenticity and real action. He feigned competence just enough to make it on to the raiding ship, but soon discovered the difference between actually being a fierce Viking warrior and only pretending. Regrettably, Vinny's reputation was so damaged at this point that it would be very difficult to repair.

Further down the road in his Viking career, Mad Hadley's excellent reputation opened many doors because people knew he could get the job done. The energetic warrior was a proven performer, and opportunity would often arise to meet reputation when the time was right. As he gained experience and became a salty veteran of raiding and pillaging, a life-changing opportunity emerged: a sleek new raiding ship coming out of the shipyards needed a captain.

Hadley updated his Viking resume, which was impressive enough, but the Viking world was highly competitive and there were many outstanding resumes in the pile. Fortunately for Hadley, Vikings talked. Those who knew Hadley also knew that he was worthy, and behind the scenes a few strings were pulled. Ultimately, his reputation carried the day, and he was awarded one of the few coveted interviews. The golden rule of reputation was a powerful force, and it could be a Viking's best friend or worst enemy.

WHO YOU KNOW?

HADLEY WAS AMBLING down the village road on his way to the captain interview when he ran into his old acquaintance Vinny. The conversation was pleasant enough as they discussed the various frivolities of Viking life, but the tone changed when Vinny found out where Hadley was going in his shiny armor and best horned helmet. In short, Vinny accused Hadley of getting the interview simply because of who he knew.

In a way, Vinny was right because Hadley did know a lot of people. He was engaging, amiable, and always willing to help others, so naturally he had a lot of friends and acquaintances in the village. However, the misguided Vinny failed to understand that it was not the fact that Hadley knew people, but it was how those people knew Hadley. The villagers not only knew him as a friend, but also a team player that often put others ahead of himself. They also knew Hadley as a reliable and competent Viking who had always taken the initiative to get things done, so it wasn't a risk to help the rising young star. If those people had known him as anything less than he truly was, they would not have pulled strings for him—especially for such an important position.

Vinny was bitter because he had also applied for the captain's job and schmoozed everyone he could have possibly schmoozed to get an interview. He was a regular walking and talking promotion of himself, and on many nights, Vinny could be found at a popular Viking night spot called Raunchy Joe's. It was the type of place where a Viking could unwind and at the same time chat with those who matter most in the world of R&P. At the center of it all, Vinny could always be found sucking up to Vikings of influence and regaling them with tales of his devotion to the craft of mayhem.

The problem was that Vinny still talked more than he acted. His raiding skills were still mediocre at best, and he was not yet a trusted warrior or sailor. The shiftless Viking hadn't taken any advanced pillaging classes or invested in his career in any other way, although he continued to brag as though he were a master of the raiding and pillaging world. Although it wasn't readily apparent to Vinny, everyone understood that his boasting was just talk followed by more talk and no action.

It didn't matter how many people Vinny schmoozed or how much he boasted because everyone knew he wasn't capable of performing as the captain of a raiding ship. Vinny was correct in assuming that connections mattered, but he didn't comprehend that he also had to be a skilled and capable warrior for those connections to matter in the way he wanted. Hadley was connected as well, but he understood that it's not just who you know, but how people know you.

GROW OR BE BLUDGEONED

ONE BIG PIECE in the puzzle of success that some Vikings missed was the value of personal growth. There were those who thought that after becoming capable pillagers they could sail to a few foreign lands, terrorize and loot the local villages, and they would be done. They could then retire to their Viking hamlet and live a life of leisure. Such was the case of Jim Bob the Bad. He was a talented and spirited young warrior who was confident that he had it made, but Jim Bob didn't understand that all Vikings faced a dangerous reality: either grow or be bludgeoned.

As his name implied, Jim Bob the Bad was a terrible and ferocious Viking warrior. He was a natural at the craft of mayhem, and merely looking into his eyes was enough to cause his adversaries to melt into a quivering puddle of fear. In his years at Havoc High School, Jim Bob was captain of the varsity battle ax team, and he lettered in both looting and mayhem. Naturally, with all of his talent, he was the big Viking on campus, and he was as popular as any young warrior could wish to be. If any Viking had a glowing future, it was Jim Bob the Bad.

Everything came easy for Jim Bob, so he never imagined that his easy ride would soon end. He made it into Norse University on a mayhem scholarship, but was slow to realize that he would have to perform at a higher level than in the past. In his young mind, it was much more appealing to continue riding his natural abilities for the foreseeable future. The future, however, is never foreseeable.

As fate would have it, Jim Bob's future dawned within the chaos of the Norse U. mayhem practice field. On the first day of mayhem practice, he swaggered onto the field with all of the pomp and arrogance he could muster, but his self-assurance didn't shield him for long. He had grown accustomed to vanquishing his opponents with a single blow, therefore Jim Bob was only half engaged when he was suddenly grounded by a thunderous blow from out of nowhere. The tremendous hit came from a young walk-on who Jim Bob had always taken for granted during high school: a Viking named Wee Hadley.

Hadley was, in fact, a late bloomer who always lacked the physical prowess of many of his classmates at Havoc High. He was short and skinny and did not seem the type who would grow into a fearsome warrior. The pint-sized Viking often struggled mightily with the physical tasks that many Vikings took for granted, but he had heart and was willing to grow—and that would change the course of his life.

Wee Hadley had quietly evolved into a formidable force, although Jim Bob was entirely unaware of this as he lay on the practice field with broken horns and a massively bruised ego.

Jim Bob vowed to exact ferocious revenge on Hadley, but failed to realize that he had been felled by more than just a lucky blow. The next day, he was once again vanquished by the bantam warrior, and once again he vowed revenge. However, the oblivious brute did nothing to grow his battle skills to meet this new challenge. He simply failed to consider that he needed to work harder and learn more. Consequently, the thrashings became a daily event, and Jim Bob was eventually beaten into a stuttering and drooling shadow of his former bad self.

Jim Bob failed to recognize that he needed to grow and gain the skill to meet his future. Instead, his future met him in a hard way. The next semester, his scholarship money was awarded to Hadley, and no one ever referred to him as Wee Hadley again.

Instead, he was now called Mad Hadley for his fervor and boldness on the mayhem field.

Hadley turned the course of his life by growing. After graduation from Havoc High, he didn't know that his future involved thrashing Jim Bob repeatedly and taking all of his scholarship money, but he did know that he had to improve in every manner possible. The tenacious little Viking studied and practiced, and then studied and practiced some more until he eventually possessed a daunting repertoire of warrior skills. Mad Hadley grew to meet his future, whereas Jim Bob did not.

Jim Bob the Bad tried a career as a freelance pillager in the real world after losing his scholarship, but he didn't fare well as his ferocious appearance was severely degraded by a droopy eye, constant drool, and the fact that he could no longer pronounce the letter "r." He should have kept growing when he had the chance, instead, he was bludgeoned into senselessness.

THE VIKING FRAME OF MIND

THE WORLD IN which Hadley, Jim Bob, and the rest of the gang grew up was fraught with danger and chaos. Vikings could be living happy and carefree one day, and the next day they could be defending their lives from any number of beastly threats. Successful Vikings possessed the right attitude toward the challenging nature of Viking life, while those with the wrong attitude ended up wounded and confused. Success or failure hinged on the Viking frame of mind.

Hadley had a neighbor growing up named Norton the Numb. From an early age, Norton was a relatively strong and intelligent child with good Viking potential. He felt very little pain, hence the name, and there was never any outward reason to doubt that he would find some measure of success in the Viking world. Sadly, Norton possessed a fatal flaw that became apparent as time went by: He approached life with the wrong frame of mind.

Whether he thought he didn't deserve success or was inwardly afraid of the challenges of Viking life, no one knew, but Norton the Numb developed a negative frame of mind from an early age. He decided he couldn't succeed, therefore, he gave up on almost everything before he even began.

As a teenager, Norton would go on Friday night pillaging parties to the next village where he would always get pummeled, and his life at Havoc High was just as demoralizing. His grades were dismal, and his social standing was pitiful, yet ironically, he was thoroughly intelligent and even likable. Norton could never get into the proper Viking frame of mind, and the results were never good as he suffered a lot of humiliation and concussions.

One starry night, Norton was walking down the road on his way to Raunchy Joe's when a heard a low growl coming from a thicket on the side of the road. He then heard another growl, and then another, and he realized that he was surrounded by a pack of vicious Norse wolves. The insecure Viking had left his sword at home because he had such little faith in his ability to use it, and thus he was armed only with pessimism and a bad attitude—and neither was going to free him from this particular jam. He stood frozen with fear and the wrong frame of mind, only mustering enough strength to unleash a shrill scream as the snarling bloodthirsty wolves closed in. Not surprisingly, his shrill scream had little effect on the situation.

The wolves tore into the defenseless Norton, and the ensuing screams of agony echoed through the landscape. Then, as the first echoes faded into the trees, a mysterious woman materialized out of the darkness, armed with a battle ax and fire in her eyes. In a raging fury, she trounced the entire pack of wolves and saved the meek lad from becoming just another roadside dinner. The pitiful Norseman's life was spared, although he still lost his right leg to the brutes.

Norton the Numb and his former right leg found themselves at the end of a cycle of defeat that stemmed from his frame of mind. Ironically, it was all in his head as he had been given everything that he needed to succeed, but he chose not to believe in his own gifts and abilities. Luckily, Norton's life was spared when someone with the proper Viking frame of mind came to his rescue. She knew that she could defeat the wolves because her attitude throughout life was one of fearlessness and confidence. Of course, she wasn't just a random Viking, she was Olga the She-Bear.

PART II

WHATEVER IT TAKES, NO MATTER WHAT IT TAKES

OLGA THE SHE-BEAR was a self-assured soul whose accomplishments were far greater than collecting a few wolf skins and saving whimpering ninnies on country roads. She was respected throughout the Viking world as a warrior and leader who was often consulted on matters of war and peace, business and economics, and almost anything else relating to Viking life. Olga was a standout in the Viking world, but what set her apart was not that she simply desired success. In truth, all Vikings desired success as much as they desired to pillage and plunder, but Olga had the will to do whatever it took—no matter how difficult—to truly succeed.

Olga knew neither nobility nor wealth as a child. She was born a simple, peasant farm girl on the outskirts of the village and seemed destined to lead a simple, peasant farm life. After all, peasant girls had led the same meager existence of milking cows and sweeping the dirt off of dirt floors for generations. Why should she be any different? Her obstacles were numerous, and it would take enormous amounts of energy and effort to get where she wanted to go, but Olga had an iron will and big ideas.

The She-Bear's dreams actually started small. She knew that she wanted a better life and that she would first need a basic education. She didn't question that fact, although she knew it would be difficult because most of the Vikings in her wretched and poor neighborhood didn't read or write, or even know what arithmetic was.

As luck would have it, there was a beacon in Olga's dark night. A wealthy warrior in the village died a few years prior and left both his fortune and book collection to start a community library. The hallowed building contained many local works along with others that had been looted from places near and far. It was a treasure trove that could provide enough knowledge to shape any willing Viking into an intellectual powerhouse.

Every week, Olga trudged miles into the village through spring rain, summer heat, and winter snow to gather piles of precious books. She started small by checking out books such as *Savages Can Read* and *One Pig, Two Pigs* to learn the basics that she knew she needed to get on course. Each and every night, the determined scholar studied by candlelight at a large slab farm table that was normally used for butchering goats. Over time, it became evident that Olga would be going somewhere, even if she didn't know exactly where.

Olga had a sister named Cecily who shared the same aspirations to break out of the bleakness, although she didn't understand that many steps had to be taken along the way. She always questioned the need to trudge through the muck and mud every week, along with the need to learn many of the things that Olga thought necessary. In fact, the reluctant little Viking probably put more effort into questioning things that shouldn't be questioned than she put into trudging back and forth for books. Cecily had the desire to succeed, as every young Viking did, but she was hesitant to take the necessary steps. Olga was willing to do whatever it took—regardless of what it was—and that was where their paths began to diverge.

OPPORTUNITY KNOCKS QUIETLY

NO ONE KNEW with exact certainty why he was called Harold the Black, but the name seemed to fit. Harold was a legendary Viking who was feared by his enemies and exalted by his peers. After an extremely successful career as a raider, he invested most of his earnings in local businesses that had all prospered. The great warrior and businessman also knew that all of the success in the world was worth nothing until a Viking gave something back, and he believed that there was no greater cause than the youth of the Norse world. This would lead to the quiet knock of opportunity for Olga and Cecily—if they were willing to both listen and act on it.

As fate would have it, young Olga and her reluctant sidekick, Cecily, had been plodding back and forth to the library along the same road that passed by Harold the Black's estate. The two small Vikings, being so heavily laden with armloads of books, did not go unnoticed by Harold. Although one seemed more energetic and motivated than the other, the great benefactor of Viking youth deemed them both to be a worthy cause.

One bright Norse morning, Olga and Cecily opened the rough-hewn door of their farmhouse to discover a package on the stoop that was adorned with bright yellow ribbon and their names. This was quite unusual as they led a life that was generally unencumbered by gifts of any sort. When they opened the parcel, they discovered two very fine goatskin backpacks with enough room to haul a month's worth of books. For Olga, this was the greatest gift in the world. While carrying armloads of books for miles was a pain, this gift meant that someone else believed in her potential along with her quest for knowledge. On the other hand, Cecily did not really appreciate the gift and failed to see any meaning in it, and that was the beginning of her misfortune.

The next day, they trekked to the library, each adorned with a beautiful goatskin backpack. That evening they returned to read their treasures by candlelight, or at least one of them read. Cecily, instead of learning and growing, decided to go to sleep early. Over time Cecily's drive for self-improvement steadily faded, but time and again Olga happily journeyed back and forth to the library with her goatskin backpack. Only occasionally would her indifferent sister still be bothered to go with her.

One day, a note arrived at their door. Inexplicably, it was an invitation for both girls to attend an open house at a prestigious local private school. Olga knew little about the school since she always thought that it was out of her reach, but despite the fact that her family couldn't afford the tuition, she decided to go anyway. Cecily didn't see the point in going because she couldn't see that it would lead anywhere. On the appointed day, Olga journeyed alone to the fancy private school that she couldn't afford.

The campus was clean, well appointed, and very refreshing for the girl who spent so much time on a dirty and dismal farm. The entire staff was well mannered and kind, but from the vantage point of the young girl, it was a very intriguing affair. Aside from satisfying her own strong curiosity, Olga didn't yet know what she was doing there. Still, she was accustomed to a dreary life and dreary talk and the school was positive and happy, and at the very least, she found a few moments of relief from her oppressive daily surroundings.

What Olga didn't know was that she passed by a very influential school board member's house on her constant treks to the library. Harold the Black was that board member, and upon noticing the dauntless young lass wandering around the school, he struck up a conversation with her about books, learning, and life in the Viking world. He even regaled her with stories of great battles and Viking adventures, and Olga relished every word and every second of the conversation. She told him of her quest for knowledge and confided in him that she sometimes didn't really know where she was going or what she was doing, but she would do whatever it took to find a better life. Somewhere in this brief encounter, amongst the cookies and tea that had been pillaged from an English merchant ship, Harold the Black heard what he needed to hear.

What Olga did not know was that her receptiveness to quiet opportunity was about to make all the difference. The Viking world had a way of meeting ambitious people halfway, and it would do so in Olga's case. Behind the scenes, a scholarship was arranged and an invitation to attend the clean and quiet private school was extended to the valiant young lady who seemed so determined to find a better life.

Opportunity knocked very quietly, but only Olga was sensible enough to hear it and bold enough to act on it. Cecily didn't hear the quiet knock, and even if she would have, the indifferent lass certainly wasn't willing to act on it. Instead, she waited for her future to come brashly through the door, but it rarely came that way for any Viking. Eventually, Cecily became a miserable hag who sold cabbages on the side of the road.

TOUGH TIMES, TOUGH TEACHERS

TO MAKE OLGA'S rise to the top sound smooth and without flaws would do a great injustice to her story. She experienced trials and tribulations along the way, but what set Olga apart was the way she responded to the struggle. She steadfastly refused to be dragged down by anything, and she was wise enough to learn from the tough times and tough teachers.

Olga experienced a number of personal struggles after arriving at the private school. She was just a poor and wretched farm wench, unwise in the ways of the world, and the simple girl struggled greatly in her new surroundings. None of the other students rushed to befriend the awkward ragamuffin who, in truth, smelled like she had just fallen off of a manure cart in front of the school. She also sported a wild and mangy mane that had rarely met a comb, and her looks were frightening even by Viking standards.

The unrefined little Viking also stumbled on the academic front. She struggled with many subjects that other students conquered quickly, and one teacher who had a mad fervor for excellence in everything hounded her relentlessly. He was known as the Gristle, and as his name implied he was tough and disagreeable, and young Olga seemed to catch the brunt of his displeasure. He nitpicked her swordsmanship and berated her pillaging skills until she almost believed him to be a monster rather than a teacher.

Fortunately, Olga had something that carried her beyond the stumbling blocks and the constant hounding of the Gristle. She wanted to grow and learn and be a better person, so she put her own sensitivity aside and realized that she did, in fact, smell like cow manure, along with the simple reality that she was not as good as her classmates in many things. Along with those realizations, the fiery little Viking also suddenly understood that she could be as good, if not better, than most of them. Thankfully, she also realized that a young Viking could bathe every day and comb her hair without doing any real harm.

The going was tough at first, but Olga stayed the course. She stayed up late to study even harder than she had done in the farmhouse of her early childhood, and she eventually earned a place on the dean's list. Not stopping there, the determined Viking also made a concentrated effort to show her peers that she could be a better person than anyone thought possible. She began to be mindful of her looks, and once again the world met motivation halfway. A few of her classmates began to help her with the basics of Viking beauty and cosmetics, and soon, Olga became an attractive Viking maiden. At the same time, she built a circle of reliable friends.

The iron-willed scholar also wanted to excel in raiding and pillaging, so she learned and practiced, and then learned and practiced some more, and her motivation did not go unrewarded. A coach from the varsity mayhem team noticed her relentless drive for self-improvement and began working with Olga until she evolved into a formidable young warrior. With focus, determination, and unbridled energy, she began to win awards in head lopping and general mayhem, and in time, she even became the Gristle's favorite student.

Olga rose up from the mire and met her challenges because she allowed her obstacles to become her greatest learning experiences. Instead of seeing the Gristle as an enemy, she chose to learn from him—even though his methods were somewhat questionable. She also learned from her peers and the world around her. Although it wasn't easy, the tough times and tough teachers eventually forged Olga into the Viking that she always wanted to be.

FIFI, THE FLUFFY-SOFT VIKING

OLGA SUCCEEDED FOR many reasons. One of the biggest reasons was that she understood the difference between being a strong performer with a solid core of skills versus being a soft and fluffy performer with no real core skills or strengths. Not understanding the difference between these two things would eventually become the downfall of Fifi, the fluffy-soft Viking.

Fifi was beautiful and lived carefree as a young girl. Born into a lifestyle that she too often took for granted, Fifi received everything she wanted through her looks, charm, or her family's money. She was very popular, and young Norse suitors waited outside of her house nearly every night. They brought flowers, large chunks of meat, and many other fine things, and Fifi reveled in it all.

Her parents constantly showered the beautiful Viking maiden with as much praise as she could absorb, but Fifi never stopped to ponder the fact that she hadn't really earned it. She didn't understand the misleading nature of false praise, nor did she think about the ease with which things happened in her life. The deluded lass actually believed she was gifted, even though she had never done anything of substance and had never been tested in battle. In reality, Fifi possessed a very soft and fluffy core of meaningless skills and misguided ideas about the real Viking world.

Even more unfortunate for Fifi, and those around her, was the fact that she became superficial and vain. She taunted anyone she considered to be a lesser person, although she didn't realize that much of her good fortune in life simply fell into her lap, and as such, it would be fleeting. The haughty girl also didn't understand that many of the people she frowned upon had begun to build a solid core of skills that would serve them well down the road. They had learned to cope with adversity and could manage the trials of Viking life, whereas Fifi hadn't faced the difficulties that build real Viking character.

Fifi's soft and fluffy core would be put to the test during her freshman year of college. A band of hooligans had been camping in the woods near Norse U., and because they were hooligans of the worst kind they would not be satisfied with simply singing songs around the campfire for very long. Inevitably, on a cool autumn night, their inner need to create bedlam awoke and they sauntered to the village and into a small college pub that was frequented by Norse U. students. Their entry into the festive establishment did not go unnoticed by any Viking, and the mood shifted from carefree to undoubtedly edgy.

The bedlam began in minutes. The hooligans came ready to rumble, and while the Vikings were caught a little off guard, the brave Norsemen fought fiercely and eventually the walls of the once jovial little pub collapsed with the strain of savage combat. Fifi was caught in the middle of the chaos, but the only response available from within her soft and fluffy core was an intense melodramatic display of blubbering and weeping.

Fifi had a boyfriend who was a dashing lad named Grunk. Grunk was thickly built and tenacious and he fought bravely to defend his beautiful maiden. Eventually, Fifi's would-be hero took a hard blow to the head and was knocked out cold. Grunk regained consciousness just in time to see the last of the hooligans defeated, as well as a striking blonde maiden standing gloriously amidst the chaos.

She stood with a fierce and proud stance that he had never observed in a Viking woman, and as Grunk regained his senses, he suddenly remembered seeing the young lady in action. He had been impressed by her quick thinking and ferocity, but the pitched battle didn't allow for more than a momentary glimpse. Now, he had time to see and liked what he saw, even though Fifi destroyed the magic of the moment with her continuous wailing and incomprehensible whimpering.

Grunk, despite his coarse and ignoble name, was neither slow nor shy, and he waded through the rubble to introduce himself to the striking, young blonde maiden named Olga. The fact that she possessed a solid core of Viking skills was far more appealing to him than Fifi's superficial looks and shallow personality, so he asked her out. After a brief Viking courtship, Grunk and Olga were married in a little stone church overlooking the village. Less than a year later, their son Hadley was born into the Viking world.

Olga became known as the She-Bear for her bold and predatory manner of fighting in the great pub battle. She would go on to live an extraordinary Viking life because she was a person of substance who had gained a solid core of useful Viking skills. Fifi, on the other hand, was so distraught by the entire experience that she melted into a whimpering shadow of the Viking maiden that she once was. In an ironic twist of fate, she was struck and killed by a runaway oxcart in front of the flattened pub. Eventually, a Super V-Mart was built on the site, and to this day, late-night shoppers swear that you can sometimes hear a sobbing, ghostly voice that sounds like it comes from a girl with a soft, fluffy core of useless ideas and meaningless skills.

PEOPLE, PEOPLE, AND PEOPLE

THE WORLD IN which Grunk lived presented many career paths. A Viking could become a brazen warrior, an oxcart driver, or even a shipbuilder, and that's what Grunk decided to be. Shipbuilding was a trade that needed to be learned hands-on, so he decided against going to college. He started as an apprentice shipwright and was learning all that he possibly could learn about ship construction. At the same time, the ambitious warrior also knew he would have to learn and understand the human element. This is where Grunk had a great advantage, because he knew the undeniable importance of people, people, and people.

Grunk knew that people made the world turn, so he made the right impressions on the right people in the village. He made it a point to get along with almost everyone, and he treated every Viking, including the lowliest street sweeper, with respect. The friendly young Viking also had a reputation for being a loyal team player who knew how to cooperate with others to get things done. He never openly berated other Vikings and was very well liked, and due to his personable manner and reputation, he eventually landed a job with a highly respected shipbuilder named Hector.

Hector had immigrated to the Norse lands from Spain a few years ago because he liked the cool weather. Even though Hector was an outsider, he quickly built a reputation in the Viking community as a first class shipbuilder. Day after day, Grunk learned everything he could possibly learn about shipbuilding from Hector. He also forged solid relationships with his Viking coworkers, and he made sure to take care of others just as much as he took care of himself. The wise young Viking also continued to learn about people. He learned how they thought and how they behaved, and he especially learned from both the victories and defeats of the people around him.

The business's reputation in the world of seafaring mayhem grew rapidly, and Hector soon needed someone to assume some of the leadership responsibilities. However, Hector needed Vikings who had people skills as well as shipbuilding skills. Many Vikings had one but not the other, although Grunk was different. He had become a capable shipbuilder who also knew about people. The good-natured Viking worked well with everyone and was highly respected, and Hector knew he could be counted on to handle the many people-related issues.

Grunk was officially made second in command of the entire business and his Viking future truly looked bright. He found his place in the Viking sun because he understood the human element in the workplace, and he now had a big office, a bright future, and a hefty paycheck to help support his family. Grunk understood that three things mattered most in the Viking world: people, people, and people.

KNOW WHEN TO JUMP SHIP

GRUNK AND HECTOR had a good time building ships together, and the young protégé learned a lot from his mentor about ship design and the ways of business. Regardless, Grunk woke up one day and realized his relationship with Hector had peaked and he was no longer growing. This put him in a difficult spot because he wanted to remain loyal to his boss, yet he needed to keep growing as a Viking to be loyal to himself. The ambitious Viking was in a position where he may have to jump ship from the shipbuilding company.

The perplexed Grunk was pondering this dilemma on a frosty Norse night as he stopped by Raunchy Joe's for a quick splash of Viking grog before going home to Olga and young Hadley. Upon entering the venerable establishment, he saw a figure in a corner booth that everyone knew and respected: Harold the Black. As usual, Harold was willing to advise young warriors if he deemed them worthy, and he had just as much faith in Grunk as he did in Olga years ago. On this night, it was clear that this young warrior was in need of Harold's wisdom.

Grunk was generally reserved, but he knew that Harold could be trusted. So he spilled his Viking guts—not in a pathetic whiney way—but in a calm, clear, and professional manner. Harold listened intently and admired the ambitious young Norseman's desire to become something more. As luck would have it, Harold had recently been pondering his business holdings and had been thinking of making some changes. Fate seemed at play as one of these holdings was a small shipbuilding enterprise that had a lot of potential if someone with the right energy and entrepreneurial spirit was at the helm.

Still, uncertainty nagged at Grunk. He had a secure job and a family, and there was a shadow of doubt in the back of his mind about his ability to run his own business. At the same time, he was also courageous and insightful, so instead of yielding to doubt and fear, he looked to the future and examined the possibilities. The would-be entrepreneur could be a spectacular success and become the Viking he wanted to be, or in the worst case, he could be sunk to the bottom of the business world. Of course, the idea of sinking wasn't entirely appealing, but the bold Viking also realized something that would settle the debate. Even if the worst happened, he still had a solid skill set and work ethic and he could recover no matter what.

The tumblers of fate clicked into place, and Grunk was able to scrape up enough money for a downpayment on the business. The Viking attorneys prepared the paperwork, and soon the unflinching and optimistic shipwright became a proud new business owner. But, there was one more task: quitting Hector.

Hector was an intelligent person, and he knew this day was inevitable, so he took the news well and gracefully wished Grunk all the luck in the Viking world. Grunk had been an invaluable employee, but Hector had also realized that their relationship as mentor and student had outgrown itself. The motivated young Viking would not be able to advance any further because Hector was not ready to give up his position or his entire business. In reality, he knew that his energetic protégé's yearning to grow without the room to do so would only be detrimental to everyone. Hector would miss him, but he understood why Grunk had to jump ship to get to where he really wanted to be.

TAKE A BREAK BEFORE
YOU ARE BROKEN

GRUNK WAS DRIVEN and focused and these were good things in the Viking world. Before long, his shipbuilding operation took shape. He met with success early on, and with every victory, the tireless entrepreneur became emboldened to push harder to make the business even more successful. Grunk, however, had a weakness that was common among Vikings: the unwillingness to take a break before being broken.

Grunk thought that there was never enough time; therefore, he saw taking breaks as wasteful. He wouldn't take an hour off during the day to decompress and rest his mind, let alone a weekend away or a relaxing vacation. Once the papers were signed on the new business, he didn't take even a minute to celebrate or take stock of the situation, and from that moment on, the determined entrepreneur did nothing except burn the midnight oil to get the business up and running in true Viking fashion.

Olga had always been supportive of the business, although lately she had been pleading with him to spend more time at home. However, in Grunk's mind, he was providing for his family's future, and he considered these early days too valuable to waste. He failed to see the value of time off for the sake of his family, let alone the fact that a little rest would actually make him more productive at work. The obsessive Viking didn't understand that he would see everything more clearly if he took a break, and that clarity would have allowed him to see that he was heading for a major blunder.

But from Grunk's perspective, his life was full of promise and success, especially since he had just reached a major milestone: the completion of the Sea Boar. This was his greatest accomplishment to date, and this would be the ship that would put his operation in the big leagues. Unfortunately, just as the Sea Boar was being made ready for sea trials, there was a bizarre accident. Grunk's sea trials captain was killed and eaten by a rancorous tiger that had escaped from the local zoo.

Feeling the pressure of time and the siren call of success, Grunk hired an old captain known as Psycho Bill as a replacement. Bill was a legendary Viking raider in his day, and as he aged, he became a sage advisor to the shipbuilding industry. Unbeknownst to Grunk, Bill had become severely cross-eyed as the result of too many head injuries, and he could no longer see far enough ahead to safely pilot a ship. Grunk was usually meticulous in vetting new employees, but he had lost his mental edge due to his grueling schedule and had failed to discern this critical detail.

The day of the sea trials arrived, yet Grunk still did not realize his mistake. He had worked hard and prepared well, but in his quest for success, he failed to take a break in order to gain perspective and clarity. In fact, his overworked and nearly burned-out Viking mind caused him to overlook a key warning sign: Psycho Bill had almost run over two fishing vessels in the harbor as they began the voyage. Along with failing to see that his new captain's eyesight was questionable, Grunk also failed to check the weather forecast. If he had, he would have noticed an enormous storm brewing just beyond the mouth of the fjord.

Psycho Bill did actually check the weather, but his failing vision caused him to overlook the fact that one of the worst storms in years was lying in wait for the unsuspecting crew.

The final stroke of folly transpired when the unwitting mariners failed to turn back because Psycho Bill saw only a blur of weather and Grunk, being over-worked and not thinking clearly, failed to realize the gravity of the situation. The Sea Boar lurched and crashed through wave after wave, and the crew acted with Viking cunning and tenacity, but from within the tempest arose a sinister wave with the sole purpose of smiting the mighty ship into the depths.

Despite their valiant efforts, the Sea Boar was lost to the icy sea and Grunk, Psycho Bill, and the entire crew were all missing and presumed dead. There had been numerous warning signs pointing to the impending disaster, but Grunk made poor decisions because he didn't understand the value of taking a break. A break would have provided the clarity to make the right decisions and to see problems coming straight at him. Likewise, doing something fun and relaxing would have allowed him to gain perspective on his life and career. Sadly, Grunk didn't take a break, so a tough break took him.

JUST ONE VIKING STEP

OLGA AND THE other Sea Boar families were in a tight spot. Their lives were turned upside down, and they were deep in the darkest woods of Viking life. This was a place from which only courageous and cunning Vikings could escape. Those who would make it out couldn't dwell on the monumental journey ahead because that would only dishearten the bravest of the brave. Their only choice was to focus on the current day, or sometimes only the current hour, and most importantly, they needed to understand that just one Viking step at a time was sometimes all that was necessary.

The disheartened Olga was now left alone with young Hadley and no visible means of support. The entirety of their financial resources had been invested in the Sea Boar, and regrettably, Olga had left Norse U. when she became pregnant. Now, she had no practical work experience, no degree or credentials, and no marketable skills. The situation was shockingly grim, yet Olga somehow knew that there was a way to rebuild her life. The intrepid warrior couldn't see the future, but she had both the optimism and the wisdom to take the first step forward.

After weighing all of her options, Olga enrolled once again in Norse U. Getting an education and raising a son sometimes presented serious difficulties, so she didn't always wake up each day with a cheery disposition. But, in spite of everything, she did wake up and take responsibility for her own destiny. Her coursework was a challenge and her financial difficulties were unbending, so she focused solely on the next step and tried not to think about the enormous amount of work to come. By doing so, Olga the She-Bear began to come alive. She excelled in Practical Pillaging and Advanced Bedlam, and she did all she could to become a model student and future Viking leader with a bright future once again.

Psycho Bill's widow was a different story. Contessa the Wailer was a cynical person who could find a negative aspect in anything. She whined, wailed, and moaned at every opportunity, and in doing so, she sabotaged her own chance to make a new start. The Wailer failed to take a single Viking step and instead blamed Grunk, Psycho Bill, and even the Sea Boar itself. She also blamed Olga for being in close proximity and sued Grunk's estate, but that came to naught since everything in the estate was sitting on the ocean floor. Contessa did not move forward, but instead became bogged down in the mire of blame.

When pessimism and finger-pointing failed to soothe her raw emotions, Contessa began to spend every night at Raunchy Joe's. While attempting to drown her misery in cheap Viking wine, the dismal wench wept and moaned with such veracity that Joe eventually banned her from the establishment. The Wailer was reduced to roaming the streets of the village with nothing except a bad attitude and a cheap bottle of wine for company. She ultimately settled under a bridge on the road out of town and was often jailed for throwing empty wine bottles at passing ox carts. Contessa the Wailer failed to take just one Viking step forward, and that made all the difference in the Viking world.

A MAP OUT OF THE DARKEST WOODS

WHILE BOTH OPTIMISM and small steps propelled Olga forward, she also needed to know where she was going. In other words, she needed a map of her expedition just as much as she needed the positive energy to take the necessary steps. Olga needed vision. This wasn't a mystical concept, but a way that Vikings created their own internal map—a map out of the darkest woods.

One starry Norse night, Olga was lying in bed while young Hadley slept in the next room. She was beginning to get over the loss of Grunk, although she was still a single mother in the darkest woods of Viking life. Thankfully, she harbored a sliver of hope about the future and had taken the first steps forward, but the wise young warrior was pondering the notion that she also needed to plot a course. Since there was no one else around to tell her which way to go, she realized that it was her—and only her—who was responsible for finding the path to her Viking destiny.

Olga had an idea about what she wanted for her future, so she went inside her mind and firmly saw herself getting to where she wanted to go. While it sounded silly to many Vikings, Olga discovered that having vision had a practical purpose. As she focused her mind on specific goals, she also began to see and understand the obstacles in her way and how to navigate around them. She defined her purpose and goals in her conscious mind, and the subconscious part of her Viking mind directed her through the twisting course.

The future luminary consciously saw herself being a top student at Norse U., and her quiet, subconscious mind told her to both study harder and become more physically intimidating. So she hit the books and hit the gym and day by day, week by week, and month by month she became the student warrior that she wanted to be, all while holding tight to her vision and never questioning what she needed to do.

Olga's dedication paid off, and after graduation she landed a job as a bedlam analyst in an up-and-coming R&P firm. She did her job well, yet the She-Bear harbored a grander vision for her life: She wanted to be a genuine fearsome Viking raider. Many thought it was foolish to give up her safe and cushy desk job to chase such a dream, but Olga was naturally undeterred. In a bold move that would define the rest of her life, the She-Bear dove headfirst into real world Viking mayhem by applying for a position on a raiding ship.

At this point, envisioning her new goal was easy, although there was much more work needed to turn the vision into reality. In the back of her mind, Olga knew that she would have to practice with her sword until she became a seemingly natural warrior. She would also have to learn the real world ways of raiding and pillaging until there was no doubt that she could hold her own in the fray. While it took some time, the She-Bear accomplished all of these things with a sense of dedication and fervor that turned many Viking heads.

Olga soon proved herself as a warrior, but the energetic and ever-evolving She-Bear eventually began to see herself as a respected Viking leader. She was an intelligent and formidable presence on the battlefield, but her subconscious mind subtly nudged her to do more if she wanted to lead other Vikings. She then dove into the books once again and took more courses from Norse U., and she learned all she could learn from the Viking leaders that she respected.

Bent on self-improvement and professional growth, Olga soon showed great promise as a leader. Eventually, the Big Chiefs couldn't help but realize her true value and abilities, and after years of hard work, training, and personal transformation, Olga became the first female captain in the history of R&P. The She-Bear eventually became a legendary leader in the raiding and pillaging world, all because she had the foresight and wisdom to follow the map out of the darkest woods.

THE GREAT GOLDEN KEY OF FLEXIBILITY

OLGA THE SHE-BEAR earned her place in a world where Vikings had to continually prove themselves. She was both fierce and notorious, and the mention of her name sent shivers down the spines of villagers near and far. Aside from being a renowned raider, she also tended to see the world differently than many old-school Vikings. Olga possessed the great golden key of flexibility, and with it she would open doors to the future.

The Viking world was evolving day by day, and Olga was savvy enough to ride the wave of change. But much to her chagrin, many of her coworkers were resistant to new ways of doing things. For them, bonking heads and creating havoc were still enough, but the wise and wily Olga sensed the future. She knew there was only one way for the Vikings to survive in a changing world: they would have to adapt to new ways of thinking.

The She-Bear knew that change was not only natural but necessary, and she had long been pondering a revolutionary idea. After a great deal of contemplation and planning, she decided to put her grand new concept to the test. One day, the innovative Viking set sail to the sunny coast of France on what appeared to be a routine R&P venture. The swords and battle axes were sharpened, the archery equipment was fine-tuned and ready, and her crew was composed of the greatest steely-eyed

Viking warriors in the land. This was going to be unlike any mission in the entire history of raiding and pillaging, and it would take more cunning and bravery than had ever been seen.

The great raiding ship settled in the waters just offshore from a large castle that looked like a promising target for havoc, and the cast of hardened warriors double-checked their armor, swords, bows, and battle axes in preparation for the ensuing chaos. However, appearances were deceiving, because battle would not come that day and chaos would not reign supreme on the shores of France. Olga, as shrewd as ever, had a new idea about Viking business. Instead of issuing the battle cry that would have initiated mayhem, she told her brave warriors to stay put. She was going ashore alone.

The crew thought she had lost her mind, and they were all sure she would not come back. But Olga was clever and unusually flexible in her thinking, and she knew that flexibility and innovation would lead to greatness. In a giant leap of faith, the She-Bear boldly vaulted into the surf and marched up to the castle entryway that would lead to a new way of doing things in the Viking world. As Olga reached the massive wood and iron door, she did something no Viking had ever done before. She knocked.

Being the She-Bear, it was still a rather loud knock, but at least it wasn't the thundering blow of a battering ram to which the French had become accustomed. It took several attempts to lure a single bewildered castle dweller to look through the slab door's peephole, and after several tense minutes of persuasion, Olga convinced the Frenchman that she only wanted to talk over a cup of tea.

They sat down to a warm and refreshing cup of tea and fine French hors d'oeuvres, and Olga began to explain her plan. She described how the Vikings could overrun the castle and take all the French treasure, but it would cost everyone dearly in one way or another. She explained that blood-curdling screams were becoming tiresome for everybody, and eventually they would drain all of France's resources—leaving nothing for future generations on either side. Olga understood that a Viking lifestyle based on greed and head bonking was unsustainable; therefore, she wanted to do something that was better for everyone.

Making a deal took some time since no one had ever done any actual negotiating, but eventually Olga purchased a shipload of fine French wine and cheese and sailed away leaving the castle intact. She had been thinking that the Norse people were growing weary of drinking the same Viking grog and eating the same Viking food, so she gambled on the notion that something new and refreshing would be welcome back home.

Upon arriving back in the Norse lands, Olga was able to sell the entire cargo to a hungry and thirsty Viking customer base for a very healthy profit. The greatest gamble of her career paid off, and thus was the beginning of a profitable and sustainable imported wine and cheese business that would eventually lead to a new way of doing business in Viking world.

There were still those who feared change and scoffed at progress, but they would only fall further behind as the new way gained momentum. The great golden key of flexibility made the difference between dying and thriving in a highly dynamic Viking world, and by using the key, Olga the She-Bear became a legend in her own time.

LES BANDITS DE TEMPS

OLGA WAS ON her way in a new direction. The Big Chiefs in the R&P firm were pleased with her idea and gave her free rein in the budding wine and cheese division. Fortune favored the bold in the Viking world, so Olga jumped into her new venture with boundless passion and energy. What she didn't realize is that her first complication was already creeping in with phantom-like stealth, and this insidious difficulty would arrive with one of her first shipments of French products. In France, it was an ancient order known as Les Bandits de Temps—the time bandits.

Since Olga was starting something new in the Norse lands, she decided to hire some young and fresh French talent who had the knowledge, excitement, and energy necessary to build the business. As the first shiploads of wine and cheese arrived, so did a young lad named Frédéric. Frédéric the Frenchman was an expert in French cuisine and he appeared to possess the same enthusiasm for the business as Olga. In reality, he only had a lot of enthusiasm for looking busy without actually accomplishing anything.

Frédéric was constantly swimming in a river of V-Mails and meetings in an effort to appear productive. He also liked to stir endless debates about issues that had been covered time and again, and he lived for insignificant discussions over lattes at the corner café. The beguiling Frenchman was also prone to hopping from cubicle to cubicle with the sole intent of wasting his coworkers' time, all in an illusive attempt to seem useful. Frédéric was, in fact, a full-fledged member of Les Bandit de Temps, and he was a master at the art of pilfering seconds, minutes, and even hours.

At first, Olga was pleased with her new hire and she marveled at the energy he put into his job. It was no wonder, as even the most intelligent Viking bosses were frequently fooled by the cunning and stealth of Les Bandits de Temps. Their secret motto was "always busy, never productive," and this way of thinking allowed them to look fully capable and devoted—for a while. Frédéric even stayed late many nights in an effort to appear fully engaged, but as was typical of the breed, he was inattentive to the things that mattered most. Worse yet, he had mastered the time bandits' signature skill: procrastination. Like all members of the ancient order, Frédéric's days were numbered.

Both time and fate wait for neither Viking nor Frenchman, and Frédéric's day of reckoning soon arrived. Life looked good at the wine and cheese warehouse and so did Frédéric, but he failed to realize that time he wasted was time he would have to pay back. The time had come to send out a major shipment to the Super V-Mart food chain, but despite his efforts to appear competent, Frédéric had failed to do the proper paperwork to get the right products to the right store. The blunder crashed into his mind just as he sat down for his morning latte at the corner café, and, in a state of panic, he ran back to the warehouse and started barking orders to begin loading oxcarts.

The warehouse came alive in a wine and cheese flurry, and then Frédéric became even more panicked because he was accustomed to looking busy, but not actually accomplishing anything. The frazzled Frenchman had never been mentally engaged at such a high level, and his entire world became a blur. To make matters worse, he deeply feared what Olga would do to him if she found out because, after all, she wasn't called the She-Bear for nothing. Even if he escaped with his head intact, he had gained no skills and his reputation would be in tatters, leaving him no choice but to skulk back to France.

Time and fate then joined forces to collect their final dues. Olga had an idea that all was not well, so she had been watching from afar. She strolled confidently onto the warehouse floor with sword drawn, but the floundering Frenchman didn't notice the She-Bear until she was nearly on top of him. At the sight of her gleaming sword, Frédéric did the only thing he knew how to do: He fell to the floor and curled up in a whimpering ball. Upon witnessing this pitiful spectacle, Olga didn't have the heart to lop off his head, but she did summarily fire him and have him removed from the property. The time bandit then skulked back to his apartment, but having also procrastinated in paying his rent, he found himself locked out in the Norse cold.

Frédéric wandered the streets of the village hoping that Les Bandits de Temps would come to his rescue, but they were all too busy wasting someone else's time. Humiliated and alone, he decided that the only course of action was to return home, but he was still being hounded by both fate and time. He arrived at the docks only to discover that the last ship to France just departed, and he then found that every restaurant was just closing and every inn had just rented their last room. Now he was cold, hungry, and without shelter or a ride home, so once again, Frédéric did the one thing he was skilled at: He curled up in a ball and whimpered himself to sleep.

Sadly, it was a frigid Norse night, and by the time Frédéric awoke his toes were icy blue and frozen. Just as the numb, cold time bandit decided he could take no more, the dreadful hounds of time and fate loosened their vengeful grip and he was able to find passage on a ship out of town that morning. Although the ship's doctor had to amputate most of his frostbitten toes, he eventually stepped back onto French soil with a glimmer of hope that he would secure new employment. Not realizing that he had sown his own barren seeds of fate, Frédéric moved into his parent's basement and engaged in a nearly fruitless job search.

Finally, after months of searching and groveling, Frédéric was forced to accept a position as a junior armpit sniffer in the product development lab for a French deodorant manufacturer.

PART III

MAD DOG PERSISTENCE

HADLEY'S EARLY WORLD wasn't easy without a father. It was a tumultuous ride of financial difficulties and uncertainty as Olga struggled to get back on her feet. Additionally, the young Viking faced physical obstacles that could have prevented him from becoming the brazen Viking warrior that he really wanted to be. Hadley was certainly a runt in his early years, but he possessed one of the greatest of all Viking traits: mad dog persistence.

In his youth, physical tasks were often an embarrassment for Wee Hadley. Most young warriors had no problem dashing across the mayhem fields and pummeling the practice dummies at the other end, but Hadley could barely keep up with even the slowest children. When he did finally reach the dummies, the fragile half-pint barely had the strength to heft his junior battle ax. Even on the best of days, Hadley usually failed to do any real smiting. In truth, almost any physical task was a major obstacle, and this created a major dilemma since he dreamed of nothing other than becoming an official fearsome Viking warrior.

Many of Hadley's teachers tried to dissuade him from following his dreams of raiding and pillaging because of his diminutive size and lackluster abilities. They attempted to politely steer him in the direction of more "fitting" pursuits such as accounting or cooking, and many were bold enough to tell him to give up altogether because he would never make it in the R&P

world. Still, Hadley knew what he wanted, and he knew that he could somehow overcome his physical limitations. He also knew that the fearsome Viking warrior job description required certain specifications, and anyone wanting the job had to meet those specifications entirely.

Hadley was persistent and that's all that mattered. He tried out for the Havoc High Mayhem Team in his freshman year but failed. He tried again his sophomore and junior years and still failed. He never gave up, and despite failure and rejection, he still pursued his dream.

Day after day, Wee Hadley worked out doggedly. He spent hours in the woods swinging his battle ax at unyielding trees until he reached a point of absolute exhaustion. He took battering after battering while practicing with his friends, and he would often work on the basics of mayhem well into the night. After another year of hard work and diligence, Hadley boldly and optimistically showed up once again for the Havoc High mayhem team tryouts at the beginning of his senior year. Once again, he failed.

This last failure was a severe blow to the little Viking, and he moped around the village for a few weeks. Still, something inside Hadley drove him to persist, and he started practicing again. Day and night and in all kinds of weather, he trained and practiced. He acquired many black eyes and a profusion of other bruises, but finally, there came a day when Hadley had shaken off the rejection of the past. He had gained enough physical prowess and skill in the art of mayhem to walk confidently onto the Norse U. practice fields. Only now the persistent warrior had a distinct advantage. All of those years of struggle had provided him with the internal fortitude to excel—especially as the battles grew in difficulty over time.

While Hadley struggled physically, he had a classmate in the opposite boat. Feral Dave was a young farm lad who just transferred from a rural school. He was big for his age, and his size combined with a youth spent working on a farm gave him physical abilities that greatly surpassed many of his urban-bred classmates. While many of them bemoaned long practice hours and the grueling physical requirements of the mayhem team, Dave accepted the difficulty with ease and always looked ready for more.

Although he was physically gifted, Feral Dave had weaknesses of a different kind. He was highly uncivilized and not well suited to the social and academic environment of his new Viking school. He especially had trouble focusing in the classroom, and he experienced difficulties due to a particular idiosyncrasy: a bad temper that made him quick to bonk the head of anyone that offended him. Many Vikings equated his personality to that of a mangy wildcat, and accordingly, he was hung with the moniker of Feral Dave.

Dave, like Hadley, knew that if he wanted to go further in life, he would have to tackle his own weaknesses. He wanted to be a Viking captain, and he understood that his dream required more than just basic mayhem skills—he would also have to demonstrate both academic and social aptitude. Coincidentally, Dave had the same level of persistence as Hadley, and he parlayed that into overcoming his personal weaknesses.

Even though scholarly pursuits were a monumental struggle, the persistent Dave studied late into the night and took summer classes. He failed often and felt the scorn of his less-than-understanding peers, yet slowly and painfully, he overcame his educational deficiencies. He learned to read and write like a future Viking leader, and he persisted enough to conquer his fear of math and science. Progress was slow at first, but eventually Feral Dave built an academic foundation that would pave his way into the Norse U. R&P Program.

The rural refugee also worked diligently on his social shortcomings and learned that diplomacy and tact were far more effective than constant head bonking. Still, he occasionally slipped and someone ended up with a serious head wound, but he reduced this habit to a point where it became a charming

nuance of his personality rather than a continual social disturbance. Feral Dave never set the Viking world on fire with his academic prowess and he still lost his temper on occasion, but he
persisted in improving himself enough to open future doors.

Both Mad Hadley and Feral Dave persisted until they made
it to where they wanted to go. When they met obstacles, they
persisted, and when they failed again and again, they persisted
again and again. Mad dog persistence was one of the greatest
Viking traits, and it would pay off for both Hadley and Feral
Dave in their Viking futures.

BITTER FAILURE AND SWEET REDEMPTION

HADLEY AND DAVE became life-long friends. They always watched out for each other, and from their earliest days, the duo applied themselves enthusiastically to whatever task was at hand. They also continually grew and understood the supreme value of initiative in a Viking career. They still didn't understand that they would inevitably experience both the trials of bitter failure as well as the rewards of sweet redemption.

Early in their Viking careers, Mad Hadley, Feral Dave, and a crew of highly motivated warriors were sent on an expedition to confront a small tribe of ferocious Celts. The Celts, along with a few other adversaries, had not adopted the sustainable business model pioneered by Olga the She-Bear. They clung to their old habits because they desperately feared change, and by clinging to the past they wreaked havoc and created instability wherever they went. These primitive ruffians didn't understand that progress will always find a way.

The Vikings set sail to track down the rogue Celts with an optimistic attitude and an air of confidence. The salty breeze of the open sea heightened the senses of the warriors as they wondered what might come, and in the middle of the pitch black night their wondering ceased when they blundered into an enormous fleet of Celtic ships. It was an epic mistake for the small band of Vikings, but Mad Hadley, Feral Dave, and the rest of the crew fought with the spirit and enthusiasm of legendary warriors in an effort to reverse their fortunes.

Nevertheless, all the fervor in the world could not save the night, and as dawn broke, the vastly outnumbered Norsemen were forced to surrender. The brave young warriors had failed completely, and they were now prisoners of some very ill-tempered Celts.

As Mad Hadley and Feral Dave sat in the Celtic prison, they naturally lamented on meeting with such bad luck so soon in their careers. All Vikings made mistakes and all failed at some point, although defeat at such an early stage made them begin to have second thoughts about their choice of profession. Those thoughts didn't last long once they realized that they had a choice. They could focus on the unchangeable choices of the past, or they could focus on their future—specifically their escape.

Feral Dave especially didn't see much use in lamenting on the downsides of his job, even if it involved being chained to a dungeon wall and fed nothing but watery gruel once a day, so he shifted his focus to seeking potential ways out of captivity. Although Hadley's attitude about being chained to anything wasn't nearly as good as Dave's, he also understood that they needed to focus on the solution instead of the problem.

Although viable escape options seemed non-existent, Feral Dave located a small piece of wire on the floor of the cell. To the less ingenious eye it was not of much use, but to Dave, it was literally the key to freedom. After several days and a number of attempts, he fashioned the snippet of wire into a simple key that would release all of their shackles. There was still a major obstacle in the form of the massive steel cell door, along with the large cadre of seething Celtic guards lurking about; however, the Vikings were thinkers with a desire to conquer the odds.

Tensions were high as a drooling and disheveled guard unlocked the cell door and began spooning out gruel in the same way he had done every day of their captivity. When the time was right, Feral Dave made a chirp like a bird and pointed up to the ceiling, and the guard, being an unfortunate simpleton, looked up to see what he thought would be a cute little birdie. The Norsemen quickly overpowered him and stuffed a dirty Viking sock in his mouth to prevent him from yelling, and then they restrained the stunned oaf with the chains that had once bound them to the dank dungeon walls.

There were now two more guards just outside of the cell that had to be dealt with. Luckily, Hadley was of similar size and stature to the recently subdued oaf, so he hastily attired himself in the guard's clothing and continued to dish out gruel to his unchained compatriots as if nothing had happened. Once a favorable pretense of serving lunch was accomplished, his next move would be to exit the cell and join the other guards. This is where Mad Hadley needed to be quick, because his ruse would be short lived.

The guards knew there was something amiss when Mad Hadley stepped out of the cell, but their fear of personal growth had diminished their mental capacities enough to provide the few seconds that were needed. With Viking swiftness and ferocity, Hadley knocked out one guard with the gruel ladle, and he subdued the second by holding his head in the gruel bucket until he quit kicking. He then pulled the fire alarm, causing the rest of the Celtic guard staff to pour out of the prison. The easily duped simpletons huddled by the dumpster and began lighting cigarettes, but before they could blow their first smoke ring, they were overwhelmed by the newly liberated Vikings.

The fierce band of warriors then fought and overpowered the rest of the village and plundered all that they could. After the bold Vikings wrapped up their Celtic conquest, they found their faithful raiding ship moored at the dock waiting to take them and their newly acquired treasure back to the Norse lands. The intrepid warriors may have failed bitterly at the start, but fortune smiled on this gallant band because they had the intelligence and fortitude to move forward and find the sweet rewards of redemption.

CHAOS IS OPPORTUNITY

THE NORDIC SUN is sinking into the deep blue sea as the weathered raiding ship slips through the mouth of the icy mountain fjord that is home. With Mad Hadley proudly standing at the helm, the gallant crew is basking in the glory of being battered, bloody, and dirty. They fought hard and solved their own seemingly impossible dilemma, and they will soon be greeted at the docks by their friends, families, and a droopy-horned Frank. Of course, no one suspects that chaos is lurking just beyond the horizon, but for quick-thinking Vikings, it could also mean great opportunity.

The timing for a catastrophe could not have been worse. The Big Chiefs were all out of town for a Viking trade convention, and the junior warriors' main concern was celebrating the great Celtic prison break for as long as possible. Sadly, fate did not adhere to convenient timing. It was two days after the great homecoming, and droopy-horned Frank was sitting on a log outside the village counting the paltry sum he had earned from unloading the Celtic treasure. Then, without warning and with the speed of the Norse wind, a thundering horde from a distant village poured over the hills and lopped off his head with wild glee. The nasty, brutish, and smelly mob then surged through the outskirts and onto the streets of the main village with absolute savagery.

Vinny was the second Viking to meet the oncoming swarm, but he just flung his battle ax in their general direction and caused a grave foot wound to a very fierce looking warrior. The cowardly braggart then turned and ran for his life, and the other Vikings quickly realized they had to react intelligently or they would all lose their heads. Like the others, Hadley didn't care much for having his head lopped off that day, but he knew that a hasty counterattack against such a large mob of seasoned warriors had little chance of success. Curiously, the wily warrior couldn't help but notice the scent of fermented cabbage wafting through the air. The smell may have been a minor distraction to most, but to Hadley, it was opportunity within the chaos.

As fate would have it, the invaders had long ago discovered a way of fermenting cabbage into a culinary creation known as sauerkraut. In fact, sauerkraut was the only thing they ate aside from occasional roadkill, so it was little wonder that they were a raucous bunch. When Hadley smelled sauerkraut, he suddenly realized that the current marketplace in his village was saturated with excellent meat and cheese products, but it was still starving for good side dishes—and this simple realization would save the day.

Hadley spied an intense-looking warrior amongst the horde that he surmised to be their Big Chief, and he knew this sauerkraut-crazed beast of a man would be the key to opportunity. He also knew that he had to think quickly and act boldly, so he charged headlong toward the great warrior with mad fervor and a roaring battle cry like few had ever heard. The bold charge scattered the great leader's entourage, yet the mountain of a man himself did not waver and raised his sword to smite the brazen Viking into oblivion.

However, Mad Hadley had no intention of actually fighting. Instead, he stopped just short of the raging beast of a man and frantically waved a small white handkerchief. Out of sheer curiosity the barbaric chief lowered his sword, and Hadley, having precious little time, was able to outline a business plan where the invading tribe would be able to free themselves from their culinary wasteland by trading sauerkraut for tasty Norse sausages—and even some French wine and cheese. The Big Chief had long ago tired of his sauerkraut and roadkill diet, so he immediately saw the wisdom of the plan and halted the battle. Raunchy Joe's was still standing, so the new business partners retired to a corner booth where they hammered out the details of the new Sausage and Sauerkraut Free Trade Agreement.

Vikings around him were literally losing their heads, but Mad Hadley knew that the only way to survive was to see what others couldn't. His ability to do so earned him deeper respect in the Viking community, and he was soon invited to interview for a position as captain of a sleek new ship that was just coming out of the Viking shipyards. The Big Chiefs wanted a brave and bold leader that would do the vessel justice, and although Hadley was still young, he had proven himself to possess great potential and wisdom. After a successful interview, Mad Hadley became the youngest captain in the history of Viking R&P. Chaos was his great opportunity in disguise.

BITE OFF MORE THAN YOU CAN CHEW

FERAL DAVE, BEING a Viking of action and untamed strength, happily held his own in the village battle. He fought well and thought quickly, yet afterward he felt something was amiss. Becoming a Viking captain was his personal obsession, but after witnessing Mad Hadley's bold display he knew that he needed to stand out even more. This presented a dilemma, because standing out in the highly competitive Viking world was very, very difficult. Although he didn't understand it at the moment, Feral Dave needed to bite off more than he could chew.

Vikings liked to explore and to be the first to conquer new things. Feral Dave was especially enthusiastic in this regard, and he wanted to undertake an adventure that would build his Viking credentials. Norse lore was filled with sailing adventures and epic battles, so what could he do that had never been done before? While pondering this question one starry night on the front porch of his house, he heard a bell in the distance, and it was coming closer.

Expecting an errant cow or goat to emerge from the darkness, Dave was taken aback when a strange long-legged creature with a humped back stepped forth. The odd beast cautiously approached the befuddled Viking, then promptly brayed and spit in his face. Not one to be put off by a little saliva, Feral Dave slipped a rope around the creature's long, curving neck and prompted it into a corral behind his house.

The next morning he consulted with his compatriots to see what could be made of the unidentified beast. The gossip from Raunchy Joe himself indicated that a merchant ship from the great southern desert had broken up on the rocks outside the village, and the humped animal, along with a myriad of valuables, was part of its cargo. Dave quickly put the pieces together. The southern desert had long been known to hold great fortunes, although getting there was another story. The sea routes were arduous and filled with all manner of hazards, including the Colossal Rabid Sea Snake, but an overland route had yet to be discovered. Feral Dave had found his big adventure.

The pioneering Norseman began to research the journey and quickly found that information on previous attempts was sparse, although he did confirm that the sandy land of ancient royalty and great pyramids would be ripe for Viking business. Regardless of the scarcity of information, Dave prepared in true Viking fashion. He plotted the most likely course and stocked up with the latest Viking survival equipment, and although he had reservations at first, he determined the hairy, spitting beast would be a suitable traveling partner. Once he had done all he could possibly do, the peculiar duo set off for the desert.

The going was smooth at the start. Feral Dave, with the cargo-laden beast in tow, saw people and sights unimaginable. They travelled with relative ease and comfort, but as they reached the dry and arid regions that marked the end of the known R&P routes, the ease waned and the difficulties set in.

Water became scarce and food was rarely available, and the scorching desert terrain was also a greater challenge than anticipated. As they slogged on, the parched warrior became increasingly distraught under the unbearable sun. The going was brutally tough even for a highly fit Viking, and at times he wondered if they were even on course—or whether they would be lost in the dunes for eternity.

As days turned into weeks, his quest seemed more and more futile. Unyielding thirst had swollen his tongue so badly that he could no longer banter with his uncomprehending hairy companion, and his hunger was so deep that he would have eaten sand had it not been for the lack of water to wash it down. The time came when the situation seamed beyond hope, and that's when Feral Dave found strength he never knew he had. The intrepid warrior simply knew that he could and would finish his quest—failure was not an option.

Their circumstances were still dire, but with Dave's newly found resolve they plodded on and on…and on. Still, even with his undying motivation and natural grit, there came a point where Feral Dave's steps faded into feeble attempts at forward motion. The beast, however, seemed to be fairing well. Upon realizing this, Dave expelled the remaining supplies from his faithful companion's humped back and took the perch for himself. They journeyed onward as the tattered and exhausted Viking entered a state of delirium.

Feral Dave was nearing total collapse when suddenly the beast raised its nose to the wind, and with a bray of joy, charged off over the sand dunes. Just as the sun dipped below the desolate horizon, Dave's great traveling companion trotted into a lush oasis surrounding a pond of clear, cool water. The beast's pitiful horned passenger slumped to the ground, and together they dipped their heads in the delightful pool.

They camped among the drifting sand and bright stars that night, thankful to be alive in such a pristine locale. Feeling relieved at his good fortune, Feral Dave fell into a deep sleep. When he awoke at dawn, the haggard norseman decided to climb the nearest sand dune to see what he could see. In his wildest dreams, Dave could not have imagined this moment. As the hard-traveled warrior reached the summit, he found himself looking down into the rich valley of ancient kings and awe-inspiring pyramids. He was instantly overwhelmed by joy, relief, and deep satisfaction.

Feral Dave took on much more than he was prepared for, and when things got tough and doubt set in, the determined warrior continued to push forward—and that's how he discovered what he was really made of. The audacious warrior found he was stronger than he thought, and his abilities were far greater than he realized. Feral Dave proved himself and solidified his Viking reputation by boldly biting off more than he could chew.

RULE AS A SERVANT, NOT A KING

WHILE DAVE WAS conquering the overland R&P route to the desert, Mad Hadley was just beginning his new adventure as a captain. He was young, brave, and on his way, and he had a taste of success sooner than most. While this was a good thing, a Viking's first taste of success can also be fraught with peril. Like many others, Hadley would have to learn some of the lessons of leadership the hard way. Specifically, he was going to have to learn how to rule as a servant, and not a king.

The Norse dawn greeted the new captain as he confidently strutted through the village streets and onto the docks. It was Hadley's first day in command of the sleek new raiding vessel named the Sea Boar II. The imposing ship was the pinnacle of Viking technology, and its new commander was ready to take charge. With his shiny new helmet and freshly polished shield, Mad Hadley enthusiastically stepped onto the deck and assumed his duties.

The ship was to set sail as soon as possible on a critical R&P mission, so his first few weeks were a hectic blur. There were provisions to be stored, weapons to be issued, and of course, the never-ending string of Viking paperwork ranging from payroll to status reports. Hadley tackled everything with his usual fervor, yet the new captain was missing something very important. He had failed to be a servant to any of his people.

In his zeal to get down to business, Mad Hadley had overlooked the part of business that mattered most. He failed to sit down and talk to his warriors about their roles on the ship and their individual ambitions, and therefore he was unable to assist anyone in growing and expanding their Viking futures. The oblivious young captain also failed to understand that his people had concerns outside of the ship as well. Many of them had upcoming weddings, birthdays, and family events that were all part of everyday Viking life. In fact, his second-in-command would soon need time off because his wife was due to have a baby.

A gloomy cloud of uncertainty began hanging over the ship because the crew had limited faith in the new captain who seemed to care so little for their needs. To his credit, Hadley sensed something was amiss, and he was wise enough to let go of his ego and seek advice. The fledgling leader privately consulted his best friend and confidant about his own apprehensions and unseen shortcomings. Feral Dave had only recently returned from his great desert adventure, but he had already spent enough time at Raunchy Joe's to have heard about the new captain who cared nothing about his people.

Of course, the opposite was true, because Hadley did care deeply about his people. He simply made a grave but innocent error in the way he conducted himself in his new position. Now that he understood the problem, he realized that he could only earn the respect of his crew by being respectful of their individual needs and aspirations. In a commendable effort to make amends, the newly enlightened captain began working in earnest to meet his warriors' personal ambitions and career goals. He made sure that everyone's needs, both on and off the ship, were met. Hadley granted an immediate leave to his second-in-command so he could be home for the birth of his child, and Feral Dave enthusiastically agreed to take his place.

The apprehension that first overshadowed the new captain's command lifted like a Norse fog on a midsummer morning.

The crew suddenly felt valued and respected as individuals, and consequently, they began to work as a team with a high degree of respect for their leader. The atmosphere on the ship became open and amicable, and suddenly the future looked bright for the Sea Boar II. All it really took was for Mad Hadley to learn the value of ruling as a servant, and not a king.

HIDDEN HAIRY LEADERS

HADLEY NOW UNDERSTOOD the value of being a servant to his people, yet there was still a mysterious force at play on his ship that he did not fully comprehend. He thought that he could steer daily operations through his officers, but for some reason, this didn't always ring true. There were those who held vast amounts of prestige and power even though they were just rank and file warriors, and one of these highly influential individuals was Elmer the Abominable Viking. He was a giant, unkempt beast of a man, and he was also a hidden hairy leader.

Elmer was a somewhat odd Norseman with savage mannerisms, but he also possessed a charismatic personality and exceptional intelligence that garnered the deepest respect of all of his shipmates. He was a brilliant teacher and natural mentor, therefore many young warriors valued his opinion and often took advice from him in matters ranging from battle tactics to problems at home. They followed Elmer with unshakeable loyalty, and that made him very powerful, regardless of the fact that he lacked any official title.

Much to his detriment, Elmer had flaws that he failed to recognize. He openly resented authority of any sort, and too often he spoke his mind without regard to diplomacy or tact. He also didn't pay much attention to his personal appearance, and looking like a wild and hairy musk ox held him back in the modern world of R&P more than he understood. Truthfully, many of the formal leaders with actual titles disregarded Elmer as inconsequential because he didn't look the part, but their assumptions would soon prove to be greatly misguided.

It was a foggy Norse morning, but nothing really seemed amiss as the crew of the Sea Boar II busily prepared for its first journey: a R&P mission to merry old England. In the past, the Vikings had targeted the noble English for old-fashioned pillaging and head bonking because they found it challenging yet profitable, but this particular mission had the purpose of healing old wounds and exploring more sustainable business ventures. All was going well as the ship was being loaded with trade goods such as sausages and smoked fish when the worst occurred: a crotchety sea hag who worked in the galley tossed a lit cigarette into a trash can, and a raging fire soon engulfed the Sea Boar II.

Chaos reigned on the dock as the ship's officers, although well intentioned, flailed about trying to organize the men to fight the inferno. They were well versed in things related to battle and sailing, but they were not prepared for a disaster of this nature. Unsurprisingly, they had little real effect on the situation. Things looked very grim as flames roared and smoke boiled from the ship's crevices, yet there was still hope in one warrior who had the cunning and bravery to respond to the disaster. Elmer the Abominable Viking charged headlong into the chaos, and the younger Vikings who had faith in this hidden hairy leader fell in behind him. With Elmer in the lead, the Vikings fought the blaze into submission with buckets of sea water and Norse ferocity.

The ship was charred, but still salvageable, and the credit could only go to Elmer the Abominable Viking. When the smoke cleared, Hadley spied the grizzled Viking standing victoriously on the deck. Suddenly, he understood the mysterious force that had been at play on the ship. He now understood that some of the most influential warriors didn't always have official titles, but they held much greater influence than was often realized. Mad Hadley now understood the vast potential power of the hidden hairy leader.

DIVIDE, THEN CONQUER

THE SEA BOAR II had been saved from total destruction, but Mad Hadley was now left with the monumental task of restoring the vessel back to seaworthy condition. He had a lot on his Viking plate with the charred ship, a crew that needed work, a wife and young family, and a looming deadline to set sail for merry old England before all of the good business opportunities were taken. It was obvious that Hadley had a lot to conquer in his Viking life, but he had to understand how to divide first.

Hadley was in a conundrum because everything was a high priority, and it wasn't clear if any particular problem was more important than the other. Certainly his family was important, but he couldn't provide for them without his ship. Then again, his crew was just as important because he couldn't fix his ship and set sail or do any sort of business without them. All of these things were tied together, and he found himself in an overwhelming tangle.

So Hadley did what he had to do. He took a break and went fishing for a few hours, even though he didn't have the time to do so. Truthfully, he didn't care much about catching fish, but he knew he needed some time away from work, regardless of everything else. The horned fisherman quietly floated in his boat staring at the fluffy white clouds migrating across the fjord, and soon his mind drifted off to a Viking happy place. Suddenly, he had a great flash of inspiration. All of his tasks and obligations were manageable, he just had to divide them cleanly and wholly from each other before they could be conquered. The recharged Viking rowed back to the village with a fresh outlook and a plan.

Like many Vikings, Hadley often tried to tackle too many things at once. But the more he took on, the less he actually accomplished. He now understood that he needed to focus on one task at a time without allowing other tasks and problems to become a distraction. Rather than thinking about status reports while working on reconstruction plans, he now only thought about reconstruction plans and nothing else. Instead of worrying about finding talented sailmakers while conducting his weekly staff meeting, he focused solely on the meeting itself. Each task was given full and unadulterated concentration, and upon putting this concept into practice, the once frazzled captain became phenomenally productive.

Hadley also knew he had to divide various parts of his Viking life from each other, especially his work life and home life. He realized that he spent much of his time and energy on personal matters while at work and that drained his focus. On the other hand, the hard-charging Viking frequently took work home when he should be relaxing and focusing on his home life, and consequently, he did not come to work properly refreshed and recharged. The wily captain also realized that many of his crew were doing the same thing, so the new order of business on the Sea Boar II was simple: Focus on work when at work, and focus on home when at home.

This was easier said than done because Viking lives were often complicated and hectic, and completely drawing a line between their two worlds was a task that might not be entirely possible. Still, they did as much as they could to separate their individual worlds, and soon the crew became more focused and energetic—and life on the Sea Boar II became streamlined and smooth. Vikings who dealt less with work issues at home came to the docks refreshed and recharged, and the Vikings who no longer worried about home issues while at work were more productive and happy. Morale was soon at an all-time high.

The Sea Boar II began to spring back to life with this newly found sense of energy and focus. New masts were erected and burned timbers were repaired. Rigging and sails rose skyward, and the last vestiges of the great disaster were wiped away until one day the great vessel looked shiny new. Many Viking families also sprang back to life, and the crew became more loyal and invested in the ship and its future. Once Mad Hadley and his crew learned the importance of dividing the individual elements of Viking life, they were able to conquer everything.

THE DREADED C AND C

HADLEY AND HIS compatriots experienced a major setback when the Sea Boar II caught fire, but in reality, setbacks happened to all Vikings on occasion. Most knew how to focus and move forward, and just as important, they didn't get bogged down by the most dreaded disease in the Viking world. It was an insidious malady that dragged down many a good Viking, and it was known as C and C, or Criticizing and Complaining.

In reality, every Viking criticized and complained now and then, and some of them even had legitimate grievances that needed to be addressed. Unfortunately, there were those who started but could not stop. It would begin with complaining about the small difficulties in one's job, and soon every problem would become a major drama. Next, the Viking would move on to criticizing his boss—along with everyone else—for all of their faults and mistakes. Inevitably, the disease would intensify over time, and the Viking would grow old and bitter while being engulfed by the dreaded C and C. The most common side effects were an acute lack of success and poor quality of life.

Hence, we have the story within the story of the rebuilding of the Sea Boar II. As the damaged ship evolved from a smoking hull into a seaworthy vessel, it became apparent that new sails would be needed. As fate would have it, there were two very talented sailmakers in the village known as the Rizzotti twins.

The twins were the sons of an Italian immigrant named Guiseppe Rizzotti. Guiseppe had been lost at sea, and having been picked up by a Viking ship, he decided to stay in the Norse lands. The peculiar refugee's presence became a mixed blessing in the eyes of the Vikings. The local restaurant scene improved dramatically after he opened an Italian restaurant down by Raunchy Joe's, although the Norsemen still didn't know what to think of the verbose immigrant who spoke in two volumes: loud and louder. Cultural differences aside, Guiseppe liked the Viking life and eventually married a nice Norse maiden, and soon after, the twins were born into the Viking world.

There were widespread rumors that the Rizzotti twins were prone to the dreaded C and C. Nevertheless, Hadley was in dire need of good sailmakers, so he hired them with a glimmer of hope that the rumors were unfounded exaggerations. The first few weeks went by without incident as the craftsmen were happy to be engaged in their trade. But as time went by, the duo began to be bothered by small things that most workers on the Sea Boar II didn't even notice. It was an active place, and there was no room for foolishness or petty drama, but the Rizzotti twins did not understand this as they began to display the first symptoms. The duo also undoubtedly inherited the "loud and louder" gene, so their criticizing and complaining did not go unnoticed.

It started with complaining about the general working conditions. In truth, it was dirty and cold, but they failed to comprehend that they were working on a burned ship on the Norse docks, and the conditions were part of the job.

Complaining about the job soon evolved into criticizing Feral Dave who had been overseeing their work. In truth, Dave was a good boss and did everything he could to be a servant to his people. However, the twins were critical by nature, and as such, they were blinded to Dave's real abilities. Eventually, the criticism and complaints evolved to cover just about everything and everyone, and even Hadley became the target of the constant negativity that emanated from the Rizzotti twins.

As the C and C took over, the Rizzottis lost all perspective. They failed to realize that even though the job was sometimes difficult, all of the workers on the Sea Boar II were very well treated. Hadley provided generous pay, ample health insurance, and a flexible schedule so they could occasionally help their aging parents at the restaurant. They were also working with one of the best Viking crews in the land, and the camaraderie was unmatched anywhere, but sadly, the disease blinded them to all of this.

The twins were also blinded to the fact that Feral Dave paid attention to everything. He knew they couldn't afford any extra problems at this point, and he saw how deeply infected the twins were. The astute Viking also realized that the C and C would start to spread, but there was no easy way to solve the problem short of firing the twins.

But, after thoroughly analyzing the situation, he decided the duo had to go. It seemed brash to many on the ship because the twins were skilled sail makers and not easily replaced. However, Dave and Hadley had discussed the problem at great length and they knew that C and C could be highly contagious, so cutting off an epidemic was far more important. While it took some effort, the twins were replaced, and the Sea Boar II was restored on time and ready to make Viking history.

TO SHINE OR NOT TO SHINE

HADLEY WAS A man of character and integrity, so naturally he wanted to repay Elmer with a promotion for saving the Sea Boar II from complete destruction. Yet there was a dilemma because Elmer's outward appearance and general mannerisms prevented him from being taken too seriously by those who didn't know him well. He didn't dress well, he didn't speak well, and he emanated a particular odor that was offensive to even the roughest of Vikings. Elmer the Abominable Viking had a lot of substance but very little style, and although he didn't know it, he was at a career crossroads. To shine or not to shine, that was the question Elmer had to face.

Mad Hadley could see that Elmer wanted to become something more in the Viking world, yet he also knew that the disheveled warrior liked being himself and didn't recognize the need to change his outward appearance. How was he to convince the Abominable Viking that he had to look the part of a Viking leader if he wanted to be promoted and do the things he really wanted to do in the Viking world?

Elmer's greatest struggle was with style and shine, but the opposite was true for a young, well-groomed warrior named Percy who recently signed on to the Boar's management team. He was properly educated, well-mannered, and possessed all of the shiny armor that a young up-and-coming Norse manager would need. His horns were always sharpened, his shield was always polished, and he epitomized the expected image of a proper Viking leader. In truth, Percy looked like he just stepped off the front cover of V.Q. magazine. Yet, there was something amiss with the dapper young manager who nobody really knew, and there were those that suspected he had been hired more for style than substance. Those suspicions would soon be put to the test, because Percy, Elmer the Abominable Viking, and the Sea Boar II all had a date with destiny.

As it often did in the Viking world, fate would appear out of the deep blue fjord when it was least expected. The newly rebuilt Sea Boar II had embarked on a shakedown cruise with the sole purpose of determining if both the ship and its crew were indeed ready for the R&P mission to England. The vessel handled gracefully and cruised swiftly, and the crew performed with unerring skill. In the middle of it all, Percy commanded and delegated with every sparkling adornment on his Viking uniform in perfect order.

But the rolling waves disguised a ghastly fate, and without warning, the legendary Colossal Rabid Sea Snake broke through the surface. The two-hundred-foot-long behemoth towered over the ship with gnashing jaws and a cavernous mouth full of razor sharp fangs, and the first Viking that caught its fatal attention was the shining Percy. As the gleaming warrior looked into the melon-sized eyes of the legendary beast, the truth became apparent. He didn't have enough substance to handle this situation, and even though he looked good, he was now only a good-looking snack. Percy offered no defense beyond a dazed expression, and in a thrashing snap of sea snake jaws, the dapper warrior was gone.

There was one warrior who did have the substance to handle the Colossal Rabid Sea Snake, and the Abominable Viking sprang into action. Armed with only his sword and an unbending will, Elmer leaped onto the back of the mighty serpent and engaged in the sort of Viking combat that creates legends. The beast flailed and thrashed in the foamy sea, but the resolute warrior found an unshakeable grip among its writhing reptilian scales. Elmer was irrepressible as he clambered his way to the back of the great serpent's head, and in a legendary moment where substance met fate, the grizzled warrior thrust his sword into the gargantuan skull. The great fiend of the fjord crashed lifelessly into the blue waves from which it came, and Elmer the Abominable Viking became a true Norse hero.

This was a heroic victory, and Elmer the Abominable Viking had proven that substance trumps style when the chips are down. However, Elmer also realized something else: even the Colossal Rabid Sea Snake noticed the shiny, well-dressed warrior first. He suddenly understood that even the most substantial and skilled Vikings must be dressed appropriately to get noticed and to be taken seriously. Thus, Elmer was a changed man. Upon receiving his bonus for saving the crew of the Sea Boar II, he got a proper haircut and paid a visit to the finest tailor in the village. Nobody doubted the substance of Elmer the Abominable Viking, and now he would also have the style and presence that was also needed in the R&P world. It was time to shine or not to shine, and Elmer wisely chose to shine.

POISONED WELLS

VINNY LIVED HIS life on second chances, and he had somehow persuaded Hadley to hire him just before the shakedown cruise. He claimed to be a reformed Viking who had learned his lesson about laziness and lack of initiative, but in reality, Vinny still didn't understand anything. As fate would have it, the lackluster Viking had been the only one in a position to save poor Percy that fateful day, but he froze with fear when the Colossal Rabid Sea Snake emerged from the depths. Vinny froze because he hadn't mastered his warrior skills, and because of his personal failure, a fellow Viking was consumed by the mighty serpent. Vinny lived a life of mediocrity and laziness, and now he had completely poisoned his own well.

When the Sea Boar II returned to the docks, the shiftless Vinny was dismissed from his position and sent out into the world to find yet another job. Much to his dismay, the people who had previously forgiven and supported him would do so no longer. The Sea Snake incident sealed Vinny's reputation as an unredeemable slacker, and he was no longer trusted by anyone. He was now destitute with no job and seemingly no future, and the rock bottom Viking could no longer draw from the village's well of good will.

At long last and in his greatest moment of darkness, Vinny finally saw the light. The awakened warrior suddenly understood the folly of always pretending to work, and he finally realized the value of actually doing the work. With his newfound sense of clarity, he also understood that the only way forward was to move away from the village, and that's how he found himself with a small bag of his worldly possessions and a thumb out on the main road. Getting a ride wasn't easy at first because most of the locals knew Vinny and wanted nothing to do with him, but in time, a large, creaky wagon eased to a stop beside the haggard Viking and offered him a ride.

The driver of the wagon exuded the pungent odor of sauerkraut and seasoned pork. Vinny soon learned that the wagon belonged to the large, sauerkraut-producing Vikings who had raided the village a while back, and it was returning home from a sauerkraut and sausage trade mission. In a flash, Vinny realized that this sauerkraut wagon driver might be fate's way of meeting him halfway on his journey to rebuild his life. He settled in for the long ride to the strange new village, but what he would do when he got there, he did not know. Vinny only knew that he had to get some distance from his old life if he were to have any chance to build a new one.

Upon arrival in the new village, Vinny knew only two things. First, this would be his great new beginning. Second, the road ahead would be very tough, but he knew that he now had the knowledge and willingness to succeed. That night he camped by the side of a clear, bubbling stream and fell asleep under a blanket of bright and optimistic stars. He awoke to a new dawn, cleaned himself up, donned his best Viking suit, and doggedly started his pursuit of a new job and a new life.

Vinny still had a way with people, and the sauerkraut wagon driver had mentioned that the factory had a few open positions. Armed with nothing except optimism and a charismatic personality, he knocked on the door of the largest sauerkraut factory in the land and was led to the Viking Resources Department. At first, things didn't look good as the V.R. people seemed to have something against outside Vikings. But, after a somewhat tense interview, he was offered an entry-level position on the canning line. It wasn't glamorous or fun, but it was a fresh start. Vinny knew how to succeed this time, and he had found a fresh new well.

THE MONGOL BOSS

VINNY FOUND HIS second chance, and for once, he wouldn't take anything for granted. He now fully understood the value of initiative, hard work, and authenticity. What he still didn't fully understand is that do-overs were still a test in and of themselves, and this new working world still held some surprises of its own. At least he was now a shrewd and confident workplace warrior with the right mindset for the first challenge in his new life: the Mongol boss.

The wayward Viking's first morning at the factory was filled with the usual V.R. paperwork and general orientation, and in the afternoon he was escorted onto the factory floor where he was given a training session on his job. Vinny focused intently on learning his new duties because he knew failure was no longer an option. In fact, he was so fixated on learning that he failed to notice the icy glare coming from a catwalk above the factory floor.

The cold stare was coming from a supervisor known as the Mongol. This was more than just a nickname because, in reality, he was a genuine Mongol warrior who had roamed into the Norse lands several years ago. Rumor had it that he served with Genghis Kahn, but he was terminated for being too harsh. This was easy to believe because the Mongol was prone to fits of red-faced slobbering rage at the hint of the slightest indiscretion or problem, but he produced results and that made him an invincible authority.

The Mongol also held a long-standing grudge against the Vikings from Vinny's village. Apparently, all of the toes on his right foot were severed by a flying battle ax at the beginning of the clash against Vinny's former compatriots, and he was now embittered because he permanently walked like a wounded duck. Luckily, the short-tempered manager happened to be at the doctor's office due to his high blood pressure on the day that Vinny showed up, otherwise, the errant Norseman would have never been hired. As fate would have it though, the Mongol boss with a bad temper and deep-seated contempt was now standing between Vinny and his dream of a new life.

Soon, Vinny realized that he might not be the most popular employee, but this was his last chance. He showed up early, stayed late, and learned his job with a great Viking attitude. He took the initiative to grease the machinery and to keep things tidy on the factory floor, and he learned everything he could about the factory and sauerkraut production. The other Vikings began to take notice of Vinny's work ethic, and many of them began to respect the hard-working newcomer—a new experience for the wayward Norseman. He was building the reputation that he wanted, yet the Mongol still couldn't see through his personal bias.

The exiled Viking worked hard and did everything right, and he had proven himself to be the kind of capable and intelligent employee who would receive a fantastic performance review. In fact, he had such high hopes for his review day that he was actually looking forward to it for the first time ever. But, the tyrannical boss was not in a generous mood, and Vinny suffered the brunt of his wrath. It didn't seem fair that a Viking who tried so hard to do everything right would have such a major stumbling block set directly in his path, but at least he was smarter and wiser from his past mistakes.

Vinny could have felt angry and dejected, and he could have become just another disgruntled sauerkraut factory worker. But this was a new Vinny, so he decided to study this great obstacle rather than simply giving up. He observed his boss from afar and tried to get inside his head to think what he thought. However, he wasn't learning about the Mongol's likes or dislikes in order to discover ways of sucking up. Instead, he was learning what his boss needed and wanted from his employees. The born-again workplace warrior was trying to see the factory through the Mongol's eyes in order to discover the problems that his boss was facing.

As soon as Vinny began to see the factory from his boss's perspective, he saw an entirely different world. He saw the petty squabbles and workplace drama, and he especially saw that many of the workers failed to hold themselves accountable for their own actions. When anything went wrong, the Mongol was forced to sort through lies and finger pointing instead of relying on the honesty and integrity of his people. Consequently, it was very difficult to solve problems and prevent future mistakes, and suddenly, Vinny knew why his boss had high blood pressure.

As they often did, fate and opportunity came knocking together in mysterious disguise. It was a day like any other, and the factory was humming along with perfect ease. Vinny was doing his job well, but no Viking was perfect, and he accidentally flipped the wrong switch at the wrong time. The entire production line came to a grinding and screeching halt, and as bottles crashed to the floor and sauerkraut oozed onto the machinery, things looked very bad for the hapless Viking. It was an epic blunder, but in all fairness, the switches were labeled in a confusing manner. But, instead of making excuses or lying, Vinny gracefully faced up to his own mistake. To everyone's surprise, the Mongol did not go into a red-faced slobbering rage. Instead, he thanked the brave Viking for being honest and accountable.

The following day, Vinny took the initiative to label the switches correctly so the same thing wouldn't happen again. Upon seeing this, along with the previous day's display of integrity, the Mongol finally admitted to himself that the enthusiastic Viking was indeed a valuable asset. The next performance review found Vinny basking in the golden light of praise from the Mongol, and soon after, the do-over Viking was promoted to shift manager.

Vinny succeeded because he didn't become bitter or resentful toward his boss. Instead, he made the effort to see the factory from the Mongol's viewpoint. He learned to think beyond himself, and he made sure to be an honest and trustworthy employee that could always be relied on to do the right thing. Once he solved the problem of the Mongol boss, Vinny the Viking began a steadfast climb up the rungs of the sauerkraut ladder.

VIKING DREAMS OF GREATER THINGS

VINNY HAD HIS do-over, although he didn't have what most Vikings would consider a dream job. Still, he woke up every day, ate his Viking breakfast, put on his sauerkraut making uniform, and enthusiastically went to work at the factory. Regardless of whether his current job was glamorous or not, Vinny realized something that would ultimately be the key to his success: Viking dreams of greater things happened one step at a time, and they only happened by embracing one's current job.

Although the workplace warrior couldn't say he was fond of everything about his job, he did his best to focus on the positive aspects of his work. He was enamored by the machines and the technology of the factory, and he was always amazed that a head of cabbage could come in one door and go out another as a tasty jar of sauerkraut. Vinny also liked the people in the factory, and with the exception of a few difficult characters, he was very well-liked by his coworkers.

On the opposite side of the spectrum was Lenny the Vile, and Lenny lived up to his name in every possible way. He was always bitter because he couldn't see any glory in sauerkraut, and working in the factory was certainly not his dream job. The aggrieved Viking barely found the energy to go to work, but ironically, he found enough energy to be a continual disturbance on the factory floor. Whether he was abusing company equipment or spreading vindictive rumors about his coworkers, Lenny was always acting in a vile manner.

Lenny despised the fact that Vinny had been promoted so quickly to shift manager, and there was little doubt that one day he would turn his spite on the rising Viking star. As such, no one was surprised when Lenny started a rumor about Vinny pilfering sauerkraut and selling it out of an oxcart in a village back alley. Of course, this despicable story was in no way true, although it did catch the attention of the Mongol.

Lenny, being extremely short-sighted, failed to realize that Vinny was known for his honesty and integrity, and his enthusiasm for his job especially endeared him to the Mongol. In other words, there was no way the Mongol was buying into the rumor, although he did pay attention to its source—and malicious gossip was something he despised. Lenny the Vile was now in a place where no Viking wanted to be: directly in the sights of the Mongol boss. This last effort to wreak havoc amongst the team was the last straw, and soon the great antagonist found himself on the streets looking for a new job. Due to his offensive nature, he remained unemployed for months. Eventually, Lenny the Vile was forced to become the night janitor at the Viking insane asylum.

Lenny couldn't see through his own spiteful haze in order to find the upsides of his current job, and his negative attitude drove his unbecoming behavior to the point of self-destruction. The deluded hater failed to comprehend that many Vikings found their dream jobs by doing well at stepping stone jobs, along with the fact that all jobs—even dream jobs—had both upsides and downsides.

Vinny, on the other hand, thrived because he focused on the positive aspects of his job, and in doing so, he found the energy and enthusiasm necessary to succeed. The devoted warrior was continually promoted up the sauerkraut ladder, and along the way he discovered that dream jobs come in many unexpected forms. Through a twisting course of stepping stone jobs, Vinny came to understand that Viking dreams of greater things really could come true.

EYE-GOUGING EMOTIONS

WHILE VINNY WAS finding his fresh new life, the Sea Boar II was being made ready to sail on its considerably delayed R&P mission. The ship boasted a formidable presence that had never been seen in waters near or far, and one fine, frosty Norse morning, the sleek new vessel eased out into the icy fjord with Mad Hadley at the helm. However, Hadley wasn't himself on this particular morning. In truth, he was experiencing a fury so blinding that it was as if someone had poked him straight in the eyes. This was the eye-gouging power of emotion.

Hadley wasn't angry at his crew or sad because he had to leave his family, instead he was emotionally disoriented because the nature of the mission had changed drastically. Although their destination was still the longed-for land of England, a rumor had emerged that changed their purpose to something more profound and sacred. This was not just any run-of-the-mill Viking rumor about mountains of gold or English maidens swooning over svelte Norsemen, but a rumor that could change the course of Hadley's life.

Before they set sail, a mysterious character appeared in Hadley's office. He was a trusted friend of Harold the Black, and he relayed a seemingly credible story about Hadley's father. Grunk and his crew did not go to the bottom of the ocean with the original Sea Boar, and they were possibly still alive. Once their ship sank, the crew clambered into a small life boat and drifted for several weeks. Eventually, they were picked up by an English ship, and being markedly weakened by their time at sea, the Vikings were put in shackles and imprisoned in England. In an even more cruel twist, they had been forced to work in a pot pie prison factory all of these years.

Quite naturally, this was a significant development. Not only would Mad Hadley have the chance to rescue his long-lost father, but he could also ransack the pot pie factory and save the world from mass exposure to such a bland and meaningless food. Such were his thoughts as the seafaring prowlers approached the coast of Merry Old England, but it wouldn't be merry for long if Mad Hadley had his way with those who had held his father captive so long.

It was true that Mad Hadley was sent to do business the new and pleasant way, but in light of recent developments, he began to question himself. Do those who use forced labor deserve anything less than having their heads lopped off? Does combining stew and pie crust in order to make the dreaded pot pie violate the sanctity and goodness of regular pie in a manner that deserves the severest retribution? If so, then why not yield to vengeance and engage in old-fashioned looting, pillaging, and mayhem?

The emotional part of Hadley wanted to exact revenge by doing business the old way, yet he also knew that he had to gain control of his emotions to make good decisions for everyone. As he calmed down and his mind cleared, Hadley aptly decided that they would not do business the new way, and they would not do business the old way, they would do both. Thus, a plan was made to institute the first hostile takeover with a happy ending—happy for most, anyway.

Such was the plan as the Vikings slipped unnoticed onto the beach and over the green rolling hills to the English village and the pot pie prison factory. As morning broke, the villagers awoke to the sound of a thundering horde and the sight of fast moving Viking horns silhouetted against the rising sun. As the furious throng engulfed the village, all of the inhabitants assumed they had seen their last days.

But, much to their surprise, the villagers were not completely doomed. Hadley knew he would need people who were willing to change and grow into the new Viking way of doing business, so he instructed his warriors to round up the locals, but to do no harm to any of them.

The chaos and confusion of the scene were waning when Feral Dave spied a large stone structure perched on a great hill just outside of town. It appeared to be the sinister pot pie prison factory, and soon there was no doubt as the smell of pie crust and thick stew wafted into the village. Hadley gave the signal to begin doing business the old way, and the thundering horde assailed the loathsome fortress with old school Viking savagery. They looted, pillaged, and took no prisoners because those involved in such a dishonorable and unsavory enterprise would be unable to fit into the new way of doing business.

With the ensuing pandemonium, Hadley wondered if his father could really still be alive. Just then, a familiar horned figure emerged from the smoke and chaos. It was Feral Dave, his trusted friend and business associate, and he was struggling to drag another Viking from the horrible fighting mass.

It wasn't a wounded warrior from the Sea Boar II that he had saved, but a veteran of the original Sea Boar. The man in his grasp was an older version of Hadley with a light still in his eye, but with a body that had been worn down by years of forced pot pie making. Grunk was alive and looking at his now-grown son, but the chaos of the hostile part of the takeover was no place for a grand reunion or for emotions that could blind them to the opportunities ahead.

With a clear head and his aged father by his side, Mad Hadley raised his sword and led the final charge to end the dark days of the pot pie prison factory. The father and son fought together until they had taken over the prison, but Grunk still had a score to settle. He wanted to finish the takeover the old-fashioned way by vanquishing all of the villagers and ransacking everything, but his wise son was able to convince him that it would be counterproductive to sacrifice the future for the sake of past wrongs. Instead, the villagers were assured no harm would come to them, but the mass production of stew and pie together must be stopped. He also promised to show them a better way of doing business, although they would have to learn the new sustainable Viking way.

Armed with wisdom and their love of good dessert, Mad Hadley and Feral Dave replaced the pie fillings with appropriate ingredients including apple, blueberry, and banana cream. Then, they shipped the pot pie stew fillings back to the Viking lands and canned them, thus forming the first Viking canned stew company. Although a few heads were lopped off during the hostile part of the takeover, most of the jobs were saved in England and new jobs were created in the Viking lands. Without even realizing it, the crew of the Sea Boar II had created the first Viking multinational corporation.

Had Mad Hadley lost control of his emotions at any point, he would have failed the mission. The Vikings would have ransacked and burned everything, and none of the future opportunities would have presented themselves. It would have been a tragedy for both the Vikings and the Englishmen, and in all likelihood, Hadley would have been fired from the R&P firm when he returned. Instead, he emerged victorious with his long-lost father and a grand new enterprise, all because he kept his vision clear from the eye-gouging power of emotion.

BE TRUE TO YOUR VIKING SELF

IT WAS NO surprise that Mad Hadley, Feral Dave, and the crew of the Sea Boar II all returned to a hero's welcome. The rescue of Grunk and his crew would become a Viking legend, and the new supply of canned stew allowed for long distance R&P expeditions that greatly expanded Viking trade routes. Furthermore, the abundant supply of tasty imported pies endeared Hadley and his crew to the Viking people. There was no doubt that Hadley would soon occupy one of the top spots in the Viking business world, but lately he had been pondering something: Was he really being true to his Viking self?

The day soon came when Mad Hadley was summoned to the Ivory Tower and everyone, especially Hadley, knew what the meeting was about. It was his call to the world of the Big Chiefs, and he had already devoted a lot of thought to this day. The sparkling tower beckoned the great warrior with all of its might, and within, he found the trappings of executive life waiting. There were cavernous meeting rooms with elegant furnishings, offices with grand views, and even a Viking gym. This is what he had worked for all of his life, and all he had to do was sit down at the great conference table and sign the golden contract.

Being a man of character, Mad Hadley took care of his compatriots before anything else. First, he made sure that Feral Dave was given command of the Sea Boar II. If anyone was meant to be in command of the greatest R&P vessel in the Viking world, it was Feral Dave. He then made sure the other faithful members of his crew were given promotions and raises, and finally it was his turn.

He had thought about this moment for a long time. He had seen the enormous salary and the perks of being a Viking executive over and over in his mind, and many days, that's what drove the ambitious warrior. Mad Hadley's day in the sun was here, and with diplomacy and grace, he resigned from the R&P firm.

Of course, this was not what anyone expected, but Hadley had been thinking a lot. With the new job, he would be able to buy his family a large Viking house and take them all on expensive Viking vacations and they could lead an excellent Viking life.

However, the climb was still long and the battles would be many. The schedule of an up-and-coming Viking Big Chief was jam packed and often stressful, and the travel would be extensive. Certainly, Mad Hadley was not the type of Viking to back down from a challenge, but now he had a young wife and a growing family, not to mention that he had just found his long-lost father. Hadley also realized that he already had a good house and financial security from his previous endeavors, along with the fact that there were many worthwhile challenges beyond the R&P world.

The life of a Big Chief didn't seem right for the intrepid warrior, so Mad Hadley politely declined his invitation to the Ivory Tower and took a different path. In a twist of fate that no one could have foreseen, the great warrior became the head coach of the Norse U. mayhem team. It was a seemingly quieter and less daring life, yet Hadley still exercised untold influence on the Viking world through the lives he shaped as a coach and mentor. In his new role, he taught his warriors the value of personal growth and the importance of challenging themselves, and of course, Mad Hadley continued to learn and grow himself.

Hadley soon realized that his new life was balanced and perfect and he had all the money, prestige, and satisfaction that he needed. He found a new career that was right for him, and while he found that financial security was still important, the wise Norseman also discovered the value of riches other than money. He got to know his long-lost father and raise his own family, and he eventually found ways of using his warrior skills and abilities in ways he had never dreamed possible. In the end, Mad Hadley discovered the one thing that mattered most: Be true to your Viking self.

THE SEEDS OF TIME

NORTON THE NUMB and Jim Bob the Bad became partners in the shipping business and were kidnapped by pirates off the coast of Africa. Since Norton already had a peg leg and Jim Bob had an appropriate name, they were given the opportunity to switch sides. Sadly, both of them failed to pass the Initial Pirate Entrance Exam, and they were never heard from again.

Olga the She-Bear gave up the R&P world in order to go into politics. She became mayor of the village and initiated a number of public works including a new mayhem stadium and a harbor development project that turned the village into a major trade center. She was loved and respected, but upon Grunk's return she left public life in order to make up time with her long-lost husband.

Grunk built a highly successful custom raiding ship company together with his wife. He learned how to take a break and live contentedly, although he held a grudge about his captivity for the rest of his life. He spent his remaining years building excellent ships, getting to know his long-lost family, and bonking the heads of pasty white Englishmen whenever he could find them.

The Rizzotti twins eventually took over the family restaurant and nearly went bankrupt when they found that they couldn't run a business by criticizing and complaining. They eventually recovered from the dreaded disease and lived long, happy, and loud Viking lives.

Harold the Black retired, but soon became bored with the quiet life. He then bought Raunchy Joe's and turned it into the first Viking franchise. Within a decade, there were Raunchy Joe's establishments on every known continent.

Frédéric lost his job as an armpit sniffer, and once again had to live with his family where he further pursued the art of wasting time. Eventually, he was made High Chancellor of Les Bandits de Temps, but the position paid so poorly that he was never able to move out of his parent's basement again.

The Mongol died of a stress-related heart attack a year after he promoted Vinny to shift manager.

Vinny was given the Mongol's job, and from there he continued his climb up the sauerkraut ladder. Eventually, he became Vice President of Sauerkraut Exports, married a nice maiden in his new village, and had five children. He often missed his old home, but he wouldn't have traded his new life for anything.

Morty never rose above mediocrity, and he spent his remaining days conjuring up conspiracy theories about his lack of success.

The Gristle married a nice Viking maiden who somewhat smoothed his roughshod manner, although he still challenged his students as much as possible. He eventually became headmaster of the private school where he held tight to his demanding fervor for excellence—but with the occasional smile.

Psycho Bill died in the pot pie prison before the great rescue. Ironically, his last years were some of the happiest of his life because he felt that prison was a relief after living so long with Contessa the Wailer.

Hector became the largest and most prosperous shipbuilder in the Viking world. Regrettably, he succumbed to greed and attempted to embezzle from his employees' retirement fund. He was caught and immediately tarred, feathered, packed in a crate, and shipped back to Spain.

Elmer the Abominable Viking discovered the joy of looking good and being fashionable, and eventually he left the R&P world to become the style editor at V.Q. Magazine.

Feral Dave was phenomenally successful as captain of the Sea Boar II. He was eventually called to The Ivory Tower and became president of the largest R & P firm in the Viking world. It was all worth it to Feral Dave, and he made the most of it.

Mad Hadley became the greatest coach in the history of the Norse U. mayhem program. With nine NVAA Division I Championships and scores of accolades and awards, Hadley retired as a living legend. In the end, he considered the growth and success of his young warriors to be his greatest mark on the world. Mad Hadley went a long way in Viking life, and he also went the right way for himself.